INTRODUCTIONS

to the Scripture Read in Worship

Other Books by William Sydnor

How & What the Church Teaches
Jesus According to Luke
Keeping the Christian Year
Looking at the Episcopal Church
More Than Words
The Son of God (with Edric Weld)
The Story of the Real Prayer Book
Sunday's Scriptures
Traveling the Way (with Drusilla McGowen)
Your Voice, God's Word

INTRODUCTIONS

to the Scripture Read in Worship

William Sydnor

MOREHOUSE PUBLISHING
Harrisburg, PA

Morehouse Publishing

Editorial office
78 Danbury Road
Wilton, CT 06897

Corporate office
P.O. Box 1321
Harrisburg, PA 17105

Library of Congress Cataloging-in-Publication Data
Sydnor, William.
  Introductions to the scripture read in worship/William Sydnor.
    p.   cm.
  Includes bibliographical references.
  ISBN: 0-8192-1564-3
  1. Bible—Liturgical lessons, English. 2. Reading in public worship.
  3. Lectionaries. 4. Episcopal Church—Liturgy.
  5. Anglican Communion— Liturgy.   I. Title.
BS391.2.S936   1991   91-8003
264' .34—dc20   CIP

Printed in the United States of America
by
BSC LITHO
Harrisburg, PA 17105

To
Richard Wayne Dirksen
Colleague, mentor, friend

Contents

Preface

Think of the introduction to the Scripture read in church as a sort of minor art form.

I have been composing such introductions for the services at the Washington Cathedral for years. Two influences have caused them to be shorter each year and have led me to discover this chore as a fascinating art form. The first was a letter from the Reverend Reed Isaacs that made me realize the limited yet specific area of responsibility such introductions have. But more than that, his demanding presence has sat like a threatening hawk in the high branches of my imagination above my typewriter, ever ready to swoop down with claws of judgment. The second was from a most unlikely source, a book by the composer Igor Stravinsky, *Poetics of Music*. He wrote, "The more art is controlled, limited, worked over, the more it is free. . . . Whatever diminishes constraint diminishes strength." I came to realize that the job is to *introduce*, to say very little; let God speak to the worshipers through God's Word. Avoid what someone has called "an excursion into tedium." Or as Mark Twain once put it, "Eschew surplusage."

That is what I have tried to do.

Introduction

"Deliver us from those awful introductions to the Scripture read in church! They are too long, too involved, often not too relevant, and now and then even a bit too heretical."

A justified comment.

This unfortunate situation has come about in part because those introductions were thought to be expositions and not just introductions and because some clergy pushed off on the reader the responsibility for composing them. So why not forget the whole matter? No foreword of any kind and the problem vanishes.

Unfortunately, we cannot forget. Back in the heyday of liturgical revival, this insight came out of a conference on effective worship: "An ill-formed exposition or, perhaps worse, no exposition has the potential of perversion of the ancient literature of the Bible."

This insight is right about the need for some foreword but wrong in thinking it should be an exposition. We do not need to expound or explain the reading that follows, just introduce it. The preacher will do the explaining, and, we pray, the Spirit of truth will lead hearers into all truth. Only introduction is our province.

When we think about it, the hearers of any public reading need to have enough orientation to get their minds in gear to receive that particular spoken word. Otherwise, for the first few seconds or even minutes of the reading, the hearers are engaged in a guessing game. Consider an offside example: the Gettysburg address.

With no foreword, the reader begins, "Four-score and seven years ago our fathers brought forth. . . ." Most reasonably informed people will realize what they are hearing after about six words. A C-average high school freshman hears familiar phrases—among them, "conceived in liberty"—and guesses it is the Declaration of Independence. A Hispanic carpenter who has been in this country twenty years is completely in the dark, has no idea what this is. Without an introduction, reception is likely to be limited. What is needed in order that this reading be received and appreciated by all?

The reader in this case is conscientious and wants the hearers to appreciate this historic piece, so he or she prefaces the reading with this introduction:

"This is Lincoln's Gettysburg address. It is one of the most famous and most quoted addresses of modern times. The battle of Gettysburg, a decisive federal Civil War victory in July 1863, resulted in over fourteen thousand federal casualties, and the battlefield was dedicated as a national cemetery four months later. President Lincoln delivered this address at the dedication. It is said that he wrote it on the back of an envelope enroute to Gettysburg."

All true, but much too long—almost as long as the address itself. It would be appropriate in a history class studying aspects of the Civil War or a literature class studying great addresses but not at this public meeting. It is beamed at the wrong audience.

Assume that the planner knows the makeup of the audience. It is conceivable that for many audiences the only necessary foreword would be "Lincoln's Gettysburg address." Or thinking of the mixed audience suggested above, here is all the orientation needed: "This is Lincoln's

Gettysburg address. It is one of the most famous and most quoted addresses of modern times." All of those present can now have some degree of appreciation for what they are about to hear.

Consider what an introduction is supposed to do.

People have come to church to worship God. They unquestionably need some orientation in order to appreciate the Scripture they hear. What they need, however, differs from the details appropriate in a biblical seminar or the flags to watch for that the leader of a study group might consider appropriate. What do these worshipers need to know in order that this portion of God's Word may possibly speak to them during this hour of worship?

And what the hearers need to know is influenced by the mind-set of the reader.

"Think of who you, the reader, are. You are going up to that lectern to be the voice that proclaims God's Word. You believe that something important is about to happen, and, by the grace of God, you are to be the agent in bringing it about. Think yourself out of the picture and think the voice of God in. You shed the tattered rags of self-consciousness and don the glorious apparel of a proclaiming voice in God's service."*

Most of us who read God's Word in worship succumb to the temptation to usurp the role of the Holy Spirit. The Lord promised that the Holy Spirit would lead us into all truth.

*William Sydnor, *Your Voice, God's Word: Reading the Bible in Church*, (Wilton, CT: Morehouse Publishing, 1988). The book discusses at length the importance and significance of the lector's role in corporate worship and describes the training necessary.

The temptation is to tell those in the congregation that what they are about to hear is an important insight in the Bible's developing conception of God or that here is sinful behavior that will have long consequences down the years. Do not tell them. Let them discover such truths or leave it to the preacher to inform them. Tease them into listening. Create an atmosphere of anticipation.

Consider David's initial encounter with Bathsheba. Yes, Nathan's prophecy, "the sword shall never depart from your house," was true for David until his dying day—and even after. And yes, here is both great sin and humble repentance. Leave all that to the preacher. The introduction is only intended to lead the congregation into giving the reading their full attention. Simply tell them, "Here is a very human story from the life of King David." What they get out of what they hear is up to the Holy Spirit and the Spirit's colleague-of-the-moment, the person who occupies the pulpit on that occasion.

Charles Morgan has written that "the function of an artist [painter] is to enable vision in others . . . not to tell them what their vision should be . . . the duty is not to impose his vision upon men but to open their eyes."* The people who read Scripture in corporate worship have a similar responsibility. They are enablers of another's vision of divine truth. What they say in introducing the reading should not impose their vision on their hearers. Remember, they are commissioned to help their hearers hear the

*Quoted by Mary MacDermott, *In Search of the Spirit* (New York: Ballantine Books, 1985), 200.

passage. Then they stand aside in order that the Lord's promise may come true: "The Holy Spirit, whom the Father will send in my name, he will teach you all things" (John 14:26). There is no guarantee that this will happen, but do not lock out the possibility for such an occurrence.

As is true of any Christian enterprise, there are inviting temptations. Here are two common ones I have tried hard to avoid. It is very easy to exceed one's commission and take over the role of the Spirit of truth. This happens when we tell our hearers what they ought to think about that which they are about to hear or when we presume to tell them what it means. This is the inviting role of the propagandist. Everyone is tempted to tell others what they ought to think and believe and how they ought to react to the word they are about to hear. It takes great discipline to resist the temptation to try to fill their minds with our thoughts. I hope I have not trespassed on the lawn of the Spirit of truth.

The other temptation that bedevils me is to indulge in the exhilarating practice of sermonizing. Exposition belongs to the preacher. I have found it hard to trust the preacher to do that job without my help, but I hope I have succeeded.

Another temptation continually besets the reader using these or any carefully prepared introductions. It is to give the introduction from memory in your own words. A proper introduction is intentionally brief, and the wording has been carefully chosen. *Read it as written, word for word.* When a person ad-libs, giving the gist of the prepared introduction, he or she invariably talks too long, spoiling the effectiveness of the introduction and sometimes even making the reading that follows seem ridiculously short. Believe me, this happens every time. The undesired result is, as my country grandfather used to say, as sure as frogs after a rain.

I firmly believe that, without a well-informed introduction, the Word of God heard through the distorting earphones of ignorance may completely violate the meaning of the passage from Holy Writ. Could the devil have a more effective confederate?

Lections (selected readings) for which the following introductions are provided are from the Sunday lectionary of the *Book of Common Prayer*. That lectionary for the Sundays of the church year follows the three-year cycle (Year A, Year B, Year C) that has become the regular procedure in a number of American churches.

How to Use this Book most Effectively

The material here has been written for the use of the reader at the lectern. The introductions for each service are always printed on the same page. Photocopy that page and have the lector use that copy to introduce each reading. *Do not take the book to the lectern and do not ad-lib the introduction.*

YEAR A

First Sunday of Advent

Isaiah 2:1–5
In one of the opening oracles of the prophet Isaiah's book, he foresees the time when all nations and peoples will put their enmity and hostility aside and will join in worshiping God in peace.

A READING FROM THE BOOK OF ISAIAH.

Romans 13:8–14
This is Paul's advice to fellow Christians who know that the day of salvation and judgment is always imminent.

A READING FROM THE EPISTLE TO THE ROMANS.

Matthew 24:37–44
Because we cannot know when the Lord will come again, this is Jesus' advice to those who are faithful to him.

A READING FROM THE GOSPEL OF MATTHEW.

[v. 37: Begin "Jesus and his disciples were sitting on the Mount of Olives overlooking Jerusalem and he said to them, 'As the days. . . .' "]

3

Second Sunday of Advent

Isaiah 11:1-10
Advent is a time of preparation for the coming of the Messiah whom God will send to deliver the people from sin and suffering and distress. Here the prophet describes that coming messianic age.

A READING FROM THE BOOK OF ISAIAH.

Romans 15:4-13
It is easy to become discouraged because of all the sin and suffering in the world. Because Paul's faith was grounded in Scripture, it became his reason for hope even in the face of so much evil.

A READING FROM THE EPISTLE TO THE ROMANS.

Matthew 3:1-12
John the Baptist foretold the coming of the Messiah with all the bluntness and fervor of an Old Testament prophet. Here is a summary of his message.

A READING FROM THE GOSPEL OF MATTHEW.

Third Sunday of Advent

Isaiah 35:1-10

In this poem, the prophet Isaiah describes the coming day of the Lord, which will be both a day of great blessings and a time of judgment.

A READING FROM THE BOOK OF ISAIAH.

James 5:7-10

Here is a bit of early Christian writing. It is evident that the author believes the Lord will soon come as the righteous judge. This is his advice to those who share his belief.

A READING FROM THE EPISTLE OF JAMES.

Matthew 11:2-11

John the Baptist had proclaimed the coming of the Messiah and thought Jesus was he. Now in prison, John was having second thoughts. This is what happened.

A READING FROM THE GOSPEL OF MATTHEW.

Fourth Sunday of Advent

Isaiah 7:10–17

Isaiah was a member of the court of Ahab, king of Judah. In this reading, the prophet's advice to the king on a proposed international alliance is coupled with a message of doom because of King Ahab's unfaithfulness to the Lord. This passage has become identified with the birth of Jesus.

A READING FROM THE BOOK OF ISAIAH.

[*v. 10: Omit* "Again."]

Romans 1:1–7

In the opening salutation of his epistle to the Christians at Rome, Paul gives one of the New Testament's best brief descriptions of who Jesus Christ is.

A READING FROM THE EPISTLE TO THE ROMANS.

Matthew 1:18–25

This is Matthew's account of the birth of Jesus.

A READING FROM THE GOSPEL OF MATTHEW.

Christmas Day I

Isaiah 9:2–4, 6–7
The prophet wrote this poem about the Messiah who was to come. See how his description throws light on the nature of the Lord and his mission.

A READING FROM THE BOOK OF ISAIAH.

Titus 2:11–14
This bit of Christian writing, decades after the crucifixion-resurrection, sounds like part of an early Christmas sermon.

A READING FROM THE EPISTLE TO TITUS.

Luke 2:1–14 (15–20)

THE NATIVITY STORY ACCORDING TO LUKE.

Christmas Day II

Isaiah 62:6–7, 10–12

Here are two stanzas from a longer poem. They are about the people to whom the Messiah will come.

A READING FROM THE BOOK OF ISAIAH.

Titus 3:4–7

This bit of early Christian writing sounds like part of a first-century Christmas sermon.

A READING FROM THE EPISTLE TO TITUS.

Luke 2:(1–14) 15–20

THE NATIVITY STORY ACCORDING TO LUKE.

Christmas Day III

Isaiah 52:7–10
This reading is part of a poem that might be entitled "The Lord Has Come as King." This stanza is about the effect of the herald's announcement of the Lord's arrival.

A READING FROM THE BOOK OF ISAIAH.

Hebrews 1:1–12
This early Christian treatise opens with a description of the significance of the coming of the Son of God into the world.

A READING FROM THE EPISTLE TO THE HEBREWS.

John 1:1–14
The author of the Fourth Gospel stands back from the Christmas event and views it both in relation to God's eternal purpose and humanity's response to Christ's coming.

A READING FROM THE GOSPEL OF JOHN.

First Sunday after Christmas

Isaiah 61:10–62:3

In this joyful poem, an ancient seer sings of the glad tidings of salvation to Zion. Heard at Christmastime, these words can become part of the profound joy of the Feast of the Nativity of our Lord.

A READING FROM THE BOOK OF ISAIAH.

Galatians 3:23–25; 4:4–7

With the coming of Christ, our relationship to God has changed from legalism to faith. The apostle explains what this change means.

A READING FROM THE EPISTLE TO THE GALATIANS.

[*Because verses have been skipped, change* "But" *to* "For" *in 4:4.*]

John 1:1–18

The author of the Fourth Gospel stands back from the Christmas event and views it both in relation to God's eternal purpose and humanity's response to Christ's coming.

A READING FROM THE GOSPEL OF JOHN.

Holy Name (January 1)

Exodus 34:1–8
After Moses received the Ten Commandments from God on Mount Sinai, he went down, only to find the children of Israel worshiping a golden calf. In his anger, he broke the tablets on which the commandments were written. Now Moses goes up the mountain a second time to receive the commandments from God.

A READING FROM THE BOOK OF EXODUS.

Romans 1:1–7
This reading is the salutation with which the Epistle to the Romans begins. Here we see why zeal to proclaim the Lord's name among the nations dominated Paul's whole life.

A READING FROM THE EPISTLE TO THE ROMANS.

or Philippians 2:9–13
This is part of Paul's poem about the Incarnation in which he explains why the Lord's name is highly exalted.

A READING FROM THE EPISTLE TO THE PHILIPPIANS.

[*For greater intelligibility, begin with v. 8, omitting "And" and reading "Being* found in human form Jesus humbled himself. . . ."]

Luke 2:15–21
This is the account of the naming of Jesus in the nativity story.

A READING FROM THE GOSPEL OF LUKE.

11

Second Sunday after Christmas

Jeremiah 31:7–14
This poem describes the return of the exiles to Zion.

A READING FROM THE BOOK OF JEREMIAH.

Ephesians 1:3–6, 15–19a
The Epistle to the Ephesians opens with this thanksgiving, which describes what the coming of Jesus Christ is intended to mean in our lives.

A READING FROM THE EPISTLE TO THE EPHESIANS.

Matthew 2:13–15, 19–23
This is the account of the flight of the Holy Family into Egypt.

A READING FROM THE GOSPEL OF MATTHEW.

[*v. 13: Substitute* "the Wise Men" *for* "they."]

or Luke 2:41–52
This is the only story in the gospels about Jesus' childhood.

A READING FROM THE GOSPEL OF LUKE.

[*v. 41: Substitute* "Jesus" *for* "his."]

or Matthew 2:1–12
This is the account of the Wise Men coming to worship the Christ Child.

A READING FROM THE GOSPEL OF MATTHEW.

The Epiphany (January 6)

Isaiah 60:1–6, 9

This bit of ancient poetry is filled with details we associate with the Wise Men's visit to the baby Jesus and also filled with the joy that is ours in the Epiphany season.

A READING FROM THE BOOK OF ISAIAH.

Ephesians 3:1–12

The Epiphany season rings with joy because Christ came as the Savior of all people, not just as the Messiah of the Jews. In this reading, the apostle explains this Christian truth.

A READING FROM THE EPISTLE TO THE EPHESIANS.

Matthew 2:1–12

The account of the visit of the Wise Men to the baby Jesus.

A READING FROM THE GOSPEL OF MATTHEW.

First Sunday after Epiphany

Isaiah 42:1–9

On the day on which we celebrate Jesus' baptism, this "servant poem" from Second Isaiah is most appropriate. Regardless of who the poet had in mind, the Christian identifies the Lord's servant with Jesus.

A READING FROM THE BOOK OF ISAIAH.

Acts 10:34–38

This reading is part of Peter's address to Cornelius and his household after the apostle realized that God calls Gentiles as well as Jews to be followers of the risen Lord.

A READING FROM THE BOOK OF ACTS.

Matthew 3:13–17

This is Matthew's account of the baptism of Jesus.

A READING FROM THE GOSPEL OF MATTHEW.

Second Sunday after Epiphany

Isaiah 49:1–7

This reading is one of Isaiah's servant poems. In choosing Zion as the Lord's servant, God through the prophet defines Zion's commission and ours in larger terms than we might have expected.

A READING FROM THE BOOK OF ISAIAH.

[*vv. 4–5: The text has suffered from many editors. For clarity, some scholars insert the latter part of v. 5—"for I am honored in the eyes . . . etc."— after v. 4.*]

1 Corinthians 1:1–9

Paul opens his letter to the members of the church at Corinth on a note of thanksgiving that they have been called into the fellowship of the Son of God, telling them something of what that means.

A READING FROM THE FIRST EPISTLE TO THE CORINTHIANS.

John 1:29–41

In John's Gospel, Jesus' ministry begins immediately after his baptism.

A READING FROM THE GOSPEL OF JOHN.

[*v. 13: Begin* "The next day John saw Jesus. . . ."]

Third Sunday after Epiphany

Amos 3:1–8

In this reading, Amos describes his call to be God's prophet and his irresistible compulsion to speak out in God's name.

A READING FROM THE BOOK OF AMOS.

1 Corinthians 1:10–17

The trivial bickering among the Christians at Corinth causes Paul to write his first letter to them. This is what he tells them.

A READING FROM THE FIRST EPISTLE TO THE CORINTHIANS.

Matthew 4:12–23

Jesus begins his public ministry.

A READING FROM THE GOSPEL OF MATTHEW.

Fourth Sunday after Epiphany

Micah 6:1–8

This reading is a divine-human interchange and deals with how God may best be served. The matter is finally summed up by the prophet's terse description of the behavior that is acceptable to God.

A READING FROM THE BOOK OF MICAH.

[The hearers will not be aware of the different voices unless you tell them. Before v. 6 add "Now Israel speaks." *Before v. 8 add* "Finally the prophet concludes the matter."*]*

1 Corinthians 1:(18–25) 26–31

In this reading, the apostle explains to the members of the church at Corinth that God's basis for choosing people and for using them in service is very different from that of the world.

A READING FROM THE FIRST EPISTLE TO THE CORINTHIANS.

Matthew 5:1–12

The Beatitudes are the familiar opening section of the Sermon on the Mount.

A READING FROM THE GOSPEL OF MATTHEW.

Fifth Sunday after Epiphany

Habakkuk 3:1–6, 17–19
Habakkuk, the prophet who lived in about the third century B.C., was a man of unwavering faith even in a time of famine.

A READING FROM THE BOOK OF HABAKKUK.

1 Corinthians 2:1–11
Here the apostle is seeking to make clear what the wisdom of God consists of and how it differs vastly from human wisdom.

A READING FROM THE FIRST EPISTLE TO THE CORINTHIANS.

Matthew 5:13–20
In the Sermon on the Mount, Jesus both sets his followers apart from other devout Jews and holds on to the venerable faith of their ancestors.

A READING FROM THE GOSPEL OF MATTHEW.

Sixth Sunday after Epiphany

Ecclesiasticus 15:11–20

In this reading, a wise and practical man advises his son to live prudently.

A READING FROM THE BOOK OF ECCLESIASTICUS

1 Corinthians 3:1–9

In this reading, the apostle is seeking to deal with bickering and strife within the Corinthian congregation. He sets a standard to which they and we can aspire.

A READING FROM THE FIRST EPISTLE TO THE CORINTHIANS.

Matthew 5:21–24, 27–30, 33–37

In the course of the Sermon on the Mount, Jesus raises our sights regarding Christian behavior as he contrasts life in the kingdom of heaven with the moralism of the religious teaching of his day.

A READING FROM THE GOSPEL OF MATTHEW.

Seventh Sunday after Epiphany

Leviticus 19:1-2, 9-18

All that the holy God has created should be treated with reverence. This is the underlying reason for loving one's neighbor.

A READING FROM THE BOOK OF LEVITICUS.

1 Corinthians 3:10-11, 16-23

The Old Testament Law commands that all of us love our neighbors as ourselves. In this reading, the apostle builds meaning into the self we are to love as a criterion for relations with our neighbor.

A READING FROM THE FIRST EPISTLE TO THE CORINTHIANS.

Matthew 5:38-48

In this section of the Sermon on the Mount, Jesus explains the meaning of the love-your-neighbor commandment.

A READING FROM THE GOSPEL OF MATTHEW.

Eighth Sunday after Epiphany

Isaiah 49:8–18

In this poem, God, speaking through the prophet, is addressing the discouraged Jews in Babylonian exile. Like all sufferers, they needed reassurance and hope.

A READING FROM THE BOOK OF ISAIAH.

[v. 15: Begin "Then the Lord says to them. . . . "]

1 Corinthians 4:1–5 (6–7) 8–13

In this reading, Paul tells what his dedication to Christ means and, by implication, sets a high standard for his fellow Christians.

A READING FROM THE FIRST EPISTLE TO THE CORINTHIANS.

Matthew 6:24–34

In this section of the Sermon on the Mount, our Lord touches on our attitude toward property and then discusses anxiety and trust.

A READING FROM THE GOSPEL OF MATTHEW.

[v. 24: Begin "Jesus said, No one can serve. . . ."]

21

Last Sunday after Epiphany

Exodus 24:12 (13–14) 15–18

In the Bible, a cloud-topped mountain is a place of holiness—the very presence of God. This is the setting in which Moses received the Ten Commandments—a moment of great awesomeness.

A READING FROM THE BOOK OF EXODUS.

Philippians 3:7–14

In this reading the apostle evaluates his life and tells how he has grown in an appreciation of the Lord's suffering, death, and resurrection—and in an appreciation of his own vocation.

A READING FROM THE EPISTLE TO THE PHILIPPIANS.

[v. 7: Omit "Yet."]

Matthew 17:1–9

The disciples' vision on a cloud-topped mountain was of great significance to them in their growing insight as to who their Master really was. The occasion is called the transfiguration of Christ.

A READING FROM THE GOSPEL OF MATTHEW.

Ash Wednesday

Joel 2:1–2, 12–17

In about 400 B.C. the prophet Joel sees in a locust plague the ultimate judgment of God, the Day of the Lord. His call to repent is appropriately ours on Ash Wednesday.

A READING FROM THE BOOK OF JOEL.

or Isaiah 58:1–12

God, through an unknown ancient prophet, berates his people because their worship does not result in just and righteous behavior. His message is appropriate to our thinking as we enter the season of Lent.

A READING FROM THE BOOK OF ISAIAH.

[*v. 1: Begin,* "Thus says the Lord."]

2 Corinthians 5:20–6:10

Paul, using himself as an example, explains to Corinthian Christians the discipline of life and the endurance of suffering which being a follower of Christ entails.

A READING FROM THE SECOND EPISTLE TO THE CORINTHIANS.

[*v. 20: Omit* "So."]

Matthew 6:1–6, 16–21

In the Sermon on the Mount, Jesus teaches his followers the way in which their practice of piety will be acceptable to God.

A READING FROM THE GOSPEL OF MATTHEW.

[*v. 1: Begin,* "Jesus said."]

First Sunday in Lent

Genesis 2:4b–9, 15–17, 25–3:7
This reading is an edited version of the second creation story in Genesis plus the Garden of Eden story about the origin of humanity's sinfulness.

A READING FROM THE BOOK OF GENESIS.

Romans 5:12–19 (20–21)
In this reading, the apostle contrasts the coming of Adam and the coming of Jesus Christ —the effect of each of them on those who followed them.

A READING FROM THE EPISTLE TO THE ROMANS.

[*v. 12: Omit* "Therefore."]

Matthew 4:1–11
This is the account of the temptations of Jesus in the wilderness after his baptism by John the Baptist and before he began his public ministry.

A READING FROM THE GOSPEL OF MATTHEW.

[*v. 1: Omit* "Then."]

Second Sunday in Lent

Genesis 12:1-8

This reading describes one of history's turning points. Abram obeyed the divine promptings, and the result was the Bible's whole story and the influence of Christianity on subsequent history.

A READING FROM THE BOOK OF GENESIS.

Romans 4:1-5 (6-12) 13-17

This reading is part of Paul's elaborate argument addressed to the Christians at Rome. He builds upon the religious insight of Abraham and what this can mean to Christian believers.

A READING FROM THE EPISTLE TO THE ROMANS.

John 3:1-17

This is the account of the nocturnal visit that Nicodemus paid to Jesus and what that scholarly Pharisee learned.

A READING FROM THE GOSPEL OF JOHN.

Third Sunday in Lent

Exodus 17:1–7
In this reading, we glimpse something of the bickering with which Moses had to contend in leading the Israelites from Egypt to the Promised Land.

A READING FROM THE BOOK OF EXODUS.

[*v. 7: Translate the proper names. Add* "Massah, meaning test" *and* "Meribah, meaning quarrel."]

Romans 5:1–11
Here Paul describes the blessings that are ours through faith in Jesus Christ.

A READING FROM THE EPISTLE TO THE ROMANS.

[*v. 1: Omit* "Therefore."]

John 4:5–26 (27–38) 39–42
This is Jesus' encounter with a woman by a public well in Samaria. In talking with her, he moves the discussion from her physical need for water to her deeper spiritual need.

A READING FROM THE GOSPEL OF JOHN.

[*v. 5: Begin* "Jesus came to a city. . . ."]

Fourth Sunday in Lent

1 Samuel 16:1–13

Being anointed by a prophet was a ritual of commissioning to be king. The anointing of David was the beginning of the period of Israel's greatness, which was to be projected into the future by prophesies of the coming Messiah as the "Son of David."

A READING FROM THE FIRST BOOK OF SAMUEL.

Ephesians 5:(1–7) 8–14

Here a first-century writer, using as a figure of speech goodness and light, evil and darkness, exhorts his fellow Christians to follow Christ, the light of the world.

A READING FROM THE EPISTLE TO THE EPHESIANS.

[*v. 8: Omit* "For."]

John 9:1–13 (14–27) 28–38

On the occasion when Jesus heals a blind man, the expression "Christ, the light of the world" is first used. That idea comes up repeatedly throughout the New Testament.

A READING FROM THE GOSPEL OF JOHN.

[*v. 1: Begin* "As Jesus walked. . . ."]

Fifth Sunday in Lent

Ezekiel 37:1–3 (4–10) 11–14
To the faithful remnant in Babylonian captivity, their nation seemed to be dead, a lost cause. The prophet's vision and his message inspired them and gave them hope.

A READING FROM THE BOOK OF EZEKIEL.

Romans 6:16–23
This reading is part of Paul's discussion of sin and righteousness.

A READING FROM THE EPISTLE TO THE ROMANS.

John 11:(1–16) 17–44
This reading is the account of Jesus raising Lazarus from the dead. His words on that occasion set the meaning of resurrection from the dead in bold relief.

A READING FROM THE GOSPEL OF JOHN.

Palm Sunday

Matthew 21:1–11
Here is the account of the occasion from which Palm Sunday takes its name.

A READING FROM THE GOSPEL OF MATTHEW.

[*v. 1: Begin* "When Jesus and his disciples had come near Jerusalem. . . ."]

Isaiah 45:21–25
These verses are the closing stanzas of a poem about the conversion of the nations. The poet sings of "strength," "triumph," "glory," which Christians also associate with the Lord in his passion.

A READING FROM THE BOOK OF ISAIAH.

or Isaiah 52:13—53:12
This is the last of the four "servant of the Lord" poems in Isaiah. Many of its concepts and phrases have become interwoven with the passion accounts in the gospels.

A READING FROM THE BOOK OF ISAIAH.

Philippians 2:5–11
In this passage, Paul sums up his belief in Jesus Christ.

A READING FROM THE EPISTLE TO THE PHILIPPIANS.

Matthew (26:36–75) 27:1–54 (55–66)
The account of the passion and death of Jesus Christ.

A READING FROM THE GOSPEL OF MATTHEW.

Maundy Thursday

Exodus 12:1–14a

This is the origin of the Feast of the Passover, the symbolism of which lies behind the Lord's Supper.

A READING FROM THE BOOK OF EXODUS.

1 Corinthians 11:23–26 (27–32)

This is the earliest account of the institution of the Lord's Supper. Paul wrote to the Corinthian Christians almost two decades before the first gospel appeared.

A READING FROM THE FIRST EPISTLE TO THE CORINTHIANS.

John 13:1–15

This is the only account of the Last Supper in John's Gospel. Earlier, following the feeding of the five thousand, Jesus discusses what it means to "eat the flesh of the Son of Man and to drink his blood."

A READING FROM THE GOSPEL OF JOHN.

or Luke 22:14–30

This is Luke's account of the institution of the Lord's Supper.

A READING FROM THE GOSPEL OF LUKE.

[*v. 14: Read,* "When the hour had come, Jesus took his place. . . ."]

Good Friday

Isaiah 52:13—53:12
This is the best known of the servant of the Lord poems in Isaiah. Its deep spiritual insights have lead the Church to describe the Lord's passion in its phrases.

A READING FROM THE BOOK OF ISAIAH.

or Genesis 22:1–18
The story of Abraham's willingness to sacrifice his son at God's command without losing faith in the goodness of God's eternal purposes, adds a dimension of meaning to the Lord's passion.

A READING FROM THE BOOK OF GENESIS.

[*v. 1: Omit* "After these things."）

or Wisdom 2:1, 12–24
This passage sounds like an elaboration of the thoughts of the high priest and his colleagues who were responsible for the Lord's passion and death.

A READING FROM THE BOOK OF WISDOM.

Hebrews 10:1–25
Here a New Testament writer seeks to explain the significance of the fact that the blood of Jesus was shed for us.

A READING FROM THE EPISTLE TO THE HEBREWS.

John (18:1–40) 19:1–37
THE PASSION OF OUR LORD JESUS CHRIST ACCORDING TO JOHN.

Easter Day

Acts 10:34–43
This is the first sermon Peter ever preached to a Gentile congregation.

A READING FROM THE BOOK OF ACTS.

[*v. 34: Begin with* "Peter addressed Cornelius and his household saying, 'Truly I understand. . . .' "]

or Exodus 14:10–14, 21–25; 15:20–21
This is the account of the Israelites being saved from the Egyptians at the Red Sea. The exodus was God's salvation for the Israelites just as the resurrection of Christ is the way of salvation for Christians.

A READING FROM THE BOOK OF EXODUS.

Colossians 3:1–4
Paul calls the Christian's faith in the risen Christ "being risen with Christ." This is what he meant.

A READING FROM THE EPISTLE TO THE COLOSSIANS.

John 20:1–10 (11–18)
This is John's account of what happened on that first Easter morning.

A READING FROM THE GOSPEL OF JOHN.

or Matthew 28:1–10
This is Matthew's account of what happened that first Easter morning.

A READING FROM THE GOSPEL OF MATTHEW.

Easter Evening

Acts 5:29a, 30–32
Peter and the other apostles had defied the religious authorities by preaching that Jesus had risen from the dead. They were arrested and brought before the Sanhedrin. This was Peter's defense.

A READING FROM THE BOOK OF ACTS.

[*v. 29: Omit* "But."]

or Daniel 12:1–3
This vision from the Book of Daniel is the first clear mention in the Old Testament of a resurrection of the wicked as well as the righteous.

A READING FROM THE BOOK OF DANIEL.

1 Corinthians 5:6b–8
In the Passover ritual, unleavened bread was associated with the remembrance of Israel's redemption from Egypt—a people's new start. Here, Paul transfers that ancient association to Christ's resurrection and the new start that is ours because of the risen Christ.

A READING FROM THE FIRST EPISTLE TO THE CORINTHIANS.

Luke 24:13–35
Luke's Easter evening account is significant because the ways those disciples knew the risen Lord are ours also.

A READING FROM THE GOSPEL OF LUKE.

[*v. 13: Begin* "Now on that same day, two of Jesus' followers were going. . . ."]

Second Sunday of Easter

Acts 2:14a, 22–32
This reading is part of the first Christian sermon of which we have any record. Peter is preaching on the streets of Jerusalem less than two months after the crucifixion-resurrection.

A READING FROM THE BOOK OF ACTS.

[v. 14: Read only "Peter, standing with the eleven, raised his voice and addressed them."]

or Genesis 8:6–16; 9:8–16
This is the conclusion of the flood story. With the end of the flood, new life is begun, and the regular seasons and the rainbow are constant reminders of God's sustaining providence.

A READING FROM THE BOOK OF GENESIS.

1 Peter 1:3–9
Here, approximately a generation after the crucifixion-resurrection, Peter is writing to Christians in a time of persecution. Notice how his conviction of the Lord's resurrection is central.

A READING FROM THE FIRST EPISTLE OF PETER.

John 20:19–31
This is John's account of what happened on the evening of the first Easter Day.

A READING FROM THE GOSPEL OF JOHN.

Third Sunday of Easter

Acts 2:14a, 36–47

Fifty days after Jesus' crucifixion-resurrection, Peter boldly preached the first Christian sermon on the streets of Jerusalem. Here are his concluding words and the effect of his sermon on those who heard him.

A READING FROM THE BOOK OF ACTS.

[*v. 14: Read only* "Peter, standing with the eleven, raised his voice and addressed them."]

or Isaiah 43:1–12

This poem contains the amazing spiritual insights of a prophet who lived about eight centuries before the time of Jesus.

A READING FROM THE BOOK OF ISAIAH.

[*v. 1: Omit* "But."]

1 Peter 1:17–23

In this reading, about a generation after the Lord's crucifixion and resurrection, Peter explains something of the meaning of those events to fellow Christians in Asia Minor.

A READING FROM THE FIRST EPISTLE OF PETER.

Luke 24:13–35

Luke tells us this event happened on the first Easter Day.

A READING FROM THE GOSPEL OF LUKE.

Fourth Sunday of Easter

Acts 6:1–9; 7:2a, 51–60
Here is a glimpse of the early internal problems of the Christian Church and of what lead to the first Christian martyrdom.

A READING FROM THE BOOK OF ACTS.

or Nehemiah 9:6–15
Ezra the priest was one of Israel's leaders during the time of the rebuilding of Jerusalem after the Babylonian exile. This is part of his public prayer in which he rehearses Israel's salvation history—the story of God's shepherd-like concern in choosing, delivering, guiding the people.

A READING FROM THE BOOK OF NEHEMIAH.

[v. 6: Begin "Ezra prayed: 'You are the Lord. . . .' "]

1 Peter 2:19–25
These are Peter's words of encouragement to Christians living in a time of persecution.

A READING FROM THE FIRST EPISTLE OF PETER.

[v. 19: Omit "For."]

John 10:1–10
Here is the Lord's description of his role as the Good Shepherd.

A READING FROM THE GOSPEL OF JOHN.

Fifth Sunday of Easter

Acts 17:1–15
This is a description of the evangelistic travels of Paul and Silas through Macedonia and Greece. It gives us a picture of the mixed reception they and their message received.

A READING FROM THE BOOK OF ACTS.

or Deuteronomy 6:20–25
This chapter of Deuteronomy opens with Moses giving the Israelites the first and great commandment: Love God with all your being. Now he counsels them about why to observe that commandment and how to give their children religious instruction.

A READING FROM THE BOOK OF DEUTERONOMY.

[v. 20: Begin "Moses said. . . ."]

1 Peter 2:1–10
This epistle reading is addressed to Christians in a time of persecution. In it, Peter gives his readers a challenging description of what it means to be a Christian.

A READING FROM THE FIRST EPISTLE OF PETER.

[v. 1: Omit "Therefore."]

John 14:1–14
These words are part of the Lord's upper room discourse with his disciples. They look beyond his approaching death to the significance of his resurrection to his believers.

A READING FROM THE GOSPEL OF JOHN.

[v. 1: Begin "Jesus said to them. . . ."]

Sixth Sunday of Easter
(Rogation Sunday)

Acts 17:22–31

While the New Testament contains a number of Paul's writings, this is one of the fullest accounts of his preaching.

A READING FROM THE BOOK OF ACTS.

or Isaiah 41:17–20

This is a bit of ancient lyrical poetry in which an unknown prophet sees in springs of water in a barren land evidence of God's concern for the people.

A READING FROM THE BOOK OF ISAIAH.

[*v. 17: Begin* "Thus says the Lord. . . ."]

1 Peter 3:8–18

This reading is addressed to Christians who lived in a time of persecution. It was probably read in church, so we might think of it as part of an early Christian sermon.

A READING FROM THE FIRST EPISTLE OF PETER.

[*v. 8: Omit* "in the same way."]

John 15:1–8

In Jesus' talk to the disciples in the upper room shortly before his arrest and crucifixion, he uses this word-picture from nature to describe their relationship.

A READING FROM THE GOSPEL OF JOHN.

[*v. 1: Begin* "Jesus said, 'I am the true vine. . . .' "]

Ascension Day

Acts 1:1–11

Luke was author of both his gospel and the Book of Acts. This is the way his second book begins.

A READING FROM THE BOOK OF ACTS.

or Daniel 7:9–14

Jesus characteristically referred to himself as "the Son of Man." This vision of Daniel's is the only place where the heavenly Son of Man is described in the Old Testament.

A READING FROM THE BOOK OF DANIEL.

[v. 13: Read, "one like a son of man coming on the clouds of heaven."]

Ephesians 1:15–23

The author of this epistle explains the significance of Christ's ascension to the Christians in Ephesus.

A READING FROM THE EPISTLE TO THE EPHESIANS.

Luke 24:49–53

Luke describes the Lord's ascension, his last resurrection appearance, twice—here at the end of his gospel and in the opening chapter of Acts. The promise of "power from on high"—the Lord's Spirit and continual presence—makes this an occasion of great joy.

A READING FROM THE GOSPEL OF LUKE.

[v. 49: Omit "And."]

or Mark 16:9–15, 19–20

This is Mark's account of the Lord's resurrection appearances and of his ascension.

A READING FROM THE GOSPEL OF MARK.

[v. 9: Read, "Now after Jesus rose on the first day. . . ."]

Seventh Sunday of Easter

Acts 1:(1–7) 8–14

This is Luke's account of the Lord's final resurrection appearance to the disciples.

A READING FROM THE BOOK OF ACTS.

[*If vv. 1–7 are not read, begin v. 8 with* "The risen Lord said to them, "You will receive. . . ."]

or Ezekiel 39:21–29

In this oracle, God proclaims through the prophet that Israel is the recipient of a mighty act of God that all nations shall see.

A READING FROM THE BOOK OF EZEKIEL.

[*v. 21: Begin* "Thus says the Lord. . . ."]

1 Peter 4:12–19

About a generation after Christ's crucifixion-resurrection, Christians were being persecuted for their faith. Here is a message of encouragement to those Christians.

A READING FROM THE FIRST EPISTLE OF PETER.

John 17:1–11

This is Jesus' high priestly prayer, which gives an intimate glimpse of his relation to the Father and of his deep concern for his faithful followers.

A READING FROM THE GOSPEL OF JOHN.

[*v. 1: Begin* "Jesus looked up to heaven and said. . . ."]

Day of Pentecost

Acts 2:1-11

The events of the first Pentecost catapulted the believers in the risen Christ into missionary activity. Here's the story.

A READING FROM THE BOOK OF ACTS.

or Ezekiel 11:17-20

Ezekiel's promise of restoration to exiled Israel sounds similar to the Pentecost event—a body of believers bound together by the Spirit of God.

A READING FROM THE BOOK OF EZEKIEL.

[v. 17: Omit "Therefore say." In vv. 18–20, you might consider changing all pronouns from the third person to the second (e.g., "And when you come there, you will remove. . . . etc.")]

1 Corinthians 12:4-13

Paul describes the varied gifts of the Spirit and their relation to one another.

A READING FROM THE FIRST EPISTLE TO THE CORINTHIANS.

John 20:19-23

This is John's account of what took place that first Easter evening.

A READING FROM THE GOSPEL OF JOHN.

or John 14:8-17

In Jesus' upper room discourse with his disciples at the Last Supper, here is what he said about the Holy Spirit.

A READING FROM THE GOSPEL OF JOHN.

[v. 8: Read "Philip said to Jesus."]

Trinity Sunday

Genesis 1:1—2:3

THE FIRST CREATION STORY FROM THE BOOK OF
GENESIS.

2 Corinthians 13:(5–10) 11–14

Here is the closing part of one of Paul's
epistles. This is one of the first times God, as a
threefold revelation—the Trinity—appears in
Christian writings.

A READING FROM THE SECOND EPISTLE TO THE
CORINTHIANS.

Matthew 28:16–20

This is Jesus' last appearance to his disciples
in Matthew's gospel. That gospel was written
approximately two generations after the crucifixion-resurrection. The threefold Christian
trinitarian name for God had come into common
use.

A READING FROM THE GOSPEL OF MATTHEW.

Proper 1 (Closest to May 11)

Ecclesiasticus 15:11-20

In this reading, a wise and practical man advises his son to live prudently.

A READING FROM THE BOOK OF ECCLESIASTICUS.

1 Corinthians 3:1-9

In this reading, the apostle is seeking to deal with bickering and strife within the Corinthian congregation. He sets a standard to which they and we can aspire.

A READING FROM THE FIRST EPISTLE TO THE CORINTHIANS.

Matthew 5:21-24, 27-30, 33-37

In the course of the Sermon on the Mount, Jesus raises our sights regarding Christian behavior as he contrasts life in the kingdom of heaven with the moralism of the religious teaching of his day.

A READING FROM THE GOSPEL OF MATTHEW.

Proper 2 (Closest to May 18)

Leviticus 19:1-2, 9-18

All that the holy God has created should be treated with reverence. This is the original context of the love-your-neighbor commandment.

A READING FROM THE BOOK OF LEVITICUS.

1 Corinthians 3:10-11, 16-23

The Old Testament Law commands that each of us love our neighbors as ourselves. In this reading, the apostle builds meaning into the self we are to love as a criterion for relations with our neighbor.

A READING FROM THE FIRST EPISTLE TO THE CORINTHIANS.

Matthew 5:38-48

In this section of the Sermon on the Mount, Jesus explains the meaning of the love-your-neighbor commandment.

A READING FROM THE GOSPEL OF MATTHEW.

Proper 3 (Closest to May 25)

Isaiah 49:8–18

In this poem, God, speaking through the prophet, is addressing the discouraged Jews in Babylonian exile. Like all sufferers, they needed reassurance and hope.

A READING FROM THE BOOK OF ISAIAH.

[*v. 15: Begin* "Then the Lord says to them. . . ."]

1 Corinthians 4:1–5, (6–7) 8–13

In this reading, Paul tells what his dedication to Christ means and, by implication, sets a high standard for his fellow Christians.

A READING FROM THE FIRST EPISTLE TO THE CORINTHIANS.

Matthew 6:24–34

In this section of the Sermon on the Mount, our Lord touches on our attitude toward property and then discusses anxiety and trust.

A READING FROM THE GOSPEL OF MATTHEW.

[*v. 24: Begin* "Jesus said, No one can serve. . . ."]

Proper 4 (Closest to June 1)

Deuteronomy 11:18–21, 26–28

Here Moses sternly enjoins the Israelites to keep the commandments of God and to teach them to their children.

A READING FROM THE BOOK OF DEUTERONOMY.

Romans 3:21–25a, 28

In writing to the Christians in Rome, Paul puts the keeping of God's commandments in a Christian perspective.

A READING FROM THE EPISTLE TO THE ROMANS.

[*v. 21: Omit* "But."]

Matthew 7:21–27

In the Sermon on the Mount, Jesus explains how our profession of faith attains the ring of sincerity.

A READING FROM THE GOSPEL OF MATTHEW.

Proper 5 (Closest to June 8)

Hosea 5:15—6:6

In this passage, God agonizes over sinful Israel. Think of the people's words as insincerely mouthed platitudes.

A READING FROM THE BOOK OF HOSEA.

[*Begin 5:15*, "God said. . . ."; *Begin 6:1*, "Then the people said. . . ."; *Begin 6:4*, "Thus says the Lord. . . ."]

Romans 4:13–18

This reading is part of Paul's explanation of what it means to be justified by faith.

A READING FROM THE EPISTLE TO THE ROMANS.

Matthew 9:9–13

Jesus' knowledge of Scripture is amazing. Here, in justifying his actions, he quotes Hosea to hostile Pharisees.

A READING FROM THE GOSPEL OF MATTHEW.

Proper 6 (Closest to June 15)

Exodus 19:2-8a

God's covenant is with the nation of Israel and not just with Israel's leaders. As their priests were to lead people into God's presence, so now the nation was to have that same role toward the world.

A READING FROM THE BOOK OF EXODUS.

[*v. 2: Begin* "The Israelites had journeyed. . . ."]

Romans 5:6-11

Here are words of profound comfort for all who know in their hearts that they do not do a very good job of being followers of Christ.

A READING FROM THE EPISTLE TO THE ROMANS.

Matthew 9:35—10:8 (9-15)

Jesus realized how great was the need of people to hear the good news of God's love. He moved toward beginning to meet that need with a group that ultimately became the Christian Church.

A READING FROM THE GOSPEL OF MATTHEW.

Proper 7 (Closest to June 22)

Jeremiah 20:7–13

Because of his honesty and courage in telling the leaders of Jerusalem the dire things God had revealed to him, Jeremiah the prophet was thrown into prison. This is his agonizing prayer.

A READING FROM THE BOOK OF JEREMIAH.

Romans 5:15b–19

This reading is part of Paul's explanation of the blessings of grace that are ours through Jesus Christ, in contrast to the negative inheritance that has come down to us from Adam.

A READING FROM THE EPISTLE TO THE ROMANS.

[*v. 15: Begin* "For if many died through one man's trespass—that is, Adam's—much more. . . ."]

Matthew 10:(16–23) 24–33

This is part of Jesus' instruction to the twelve before sending them out into the towns and villages of Judea to announce that "the kingdom of heaven is at hand."

A READING FROM THE GOSPEL OF MATTHEW.

[*v. 24: Begin* "Jesus said. . . ."]

Proper 8 (Closest to June 29)

Isaiah 2:10–17
Here the prophet speaks of the day of the Lord when God alone will be exalted and what this will do to human pride.

A READING FROM THE BOOK OF ISAIAH.

Romans 6:3–11
This reading is Paul's explanation of the profound meaning of baptism.

A READING FROM THE EPISTLE TO THE ROMANS.

Matthew 10:34–42
These are the closing words of Jesus' instructions to the disciples when he sent them out to preach the coming of the kingdom of God.

A READING FROM THE GOSPEL OF MATTHEW.

[*v. 34: Begin* "Jesus said, 'Do not think. . . .' "]

Proper 9 (Closest to July 6)

Zechariah 9:9–12
This reading is an oracle addressed to the people of Israel who were beginning to wonder whether the promised Messiah was ever coming. It was later quoted at the time of Jesus' Palm Sunday ride into Jerusalem.

A READING FROM THE BOOK OF ZECHARIAH.

[*v. 9: Begin* "Thus says the Lord, 'Rejoice greatly. . . .' "]

Romans 7:21—8:6
In this reading, the apostle Paul wrestles with the nature of sin that God's Law fully reveals, and he gives the Christian resolution of the problem.

A READING FROM THE EPISTLE TO THE ROMANS.

Matthew 11:25–30
These words of Jesus are probably his reaction when the disciples returned and reported their success in proclaiming the good news of the kingdom of God.

A READING FROM THE GOSPEL OF MATTHEW.

Proper 10 (Closest to July 13)

Isaiah 55:1–5, 10–13

In this joyful poem, God speaks through the prophet to the exiled Israelites and sets Israel on a larger stage than that of their own concerns.

A READING FROM THE BOOK OF ISAIAH.

[*v. 1: Begin* "Thus says the Lord, 'Ho, every one who thirsts. . . .' "]

Romans 8:9–17

This reading is a part of a longer passage in which the apostle Paul explains to his readers the great benefits that come from having been blessed with the Spirit of the risen Christ.

A READING FROM THE EPISTLE TO THE ROMANS.

[*v. 9: Omit* "But."]

Matthew 13:1–9, 18–23

This is Jesus' parable of the sower, to which the early church added its explanation of the meaning.

A READING FROM THE GOSPEL OF MATTHEW.

Proper 11 (Closest to July 20)

Wisdom 12:13, 16–19

This reading from the Apocrypha is part of a longer section on God's righteousness that the Jewish author directs to Gentile readers. In form, it is addressed to God, but it is not a prayer.

A READING FROM THE BOOK OF WISDOM.

Romans 8:18–25

This reading is part of Paul's description of life in the Spirit.

A READING FROM THE EPISTLE TO THE ROMANS.

Matthew 13:24–30, 36–43

This is Jesus' parable of the tares with the Lord's explanation, which shows it to be a parable of judgment.

A READING FROM THE GOSPEL OF MATTHEW.

[v. 24: Begin "Jesus put before them. . . ."]

Proper 12 (Closest to July 27)

1 Kings 3:5-12

Solomon succeeded David on the throne of Israel. In the early years of his reign, he was a wise and discerning king. This trait is related to a dream he had shortly after ascending the throne.

A READING FROM THE FIRST BOOK OF KINGS.

Romans 8:26-34

This reading is the middle section of Paul's chapter on life in the Spirit. He makes it clear that the Lord's Spirit is our helper in prayer as well as in work and that nothing is outside God's control.

A READING FROM THE EPISTLE TO THE ROMANS.

Matthew 13:31-33, 44-49a

Here are a number of Jesus' little parables about the kingdom of heaven.

A READING FROM THE GOSPEL OF MATTHEW.

[v. 31: Begin "Jesus put before them another parable. . . ."]

Proper 13 (Closest to August 3)

Nehemiah 9:16–20

This reading is part of a penitential psalm addressed to God in which Ezra the priest reviews Israel's salvation history.

A READING FROM THE BOOK OF NEHEMIAH.

[*v. 16: Begin* "Ezra said, O Lord God, our ancestors acted. . . ."]

Romans 8:35–39

This reading is the conclusion and climax of Paul's discussion of life blessed with the Lord's Spirit.

A READING FROM THE EPISTLE TO THE ROMANS.

Matthew 14:13–21

This is the account of the feeding of the five thousand. It is recorded six times in the four gospels. The early Christians saw it as a foretaste of the heavenly banquet.

A READING FROM THE GOSPEL OF MATTHEW.

[*v. 13: Begin* "Now when Jesus heard that John the Baptist had been killed, he withdrew. . . . "]

Proper 14 (Closest to August 10)

Jonah 2:1–9

This psalm is an interlude in the Jonah story while the prophet was in the belly of the fish. Its tone of thanksgiving sounds a bit premature because it was probably a later addition to the story.

A READING FROM THE BOOK OF JONAH.

Romans 9:1–5

Paul's epistle deals with the place of Jew and Gentile in God's eternal purpose. In this reading, Paul begins a section with this wholehearted appreciation of Israel.

A READING FROM THE EPISTLE TO THE ROMANS.

Matthew 14:22–33

This miraculous episode takes place right after the feeding of the five thousand. Some scholars think it may be a misplaced resurrection appearance.

A READING FROM THE GOSPEL OF MATTHEW.

[v. 22: Begin "Jesus made the disciples. . . ."]

Proper 15 (Closest to August 17)

Isaiah 56:1 (2–5) 6–7
This reading is part of a sixth-century B.C. poem addressed to the Israelite exiles. Its lasting value lies in the conviction of God's universal concern for all people.

A READING FROM THE BOOK OF ISAIAH.

Romans 11:13–15, 29–32
In biblical times, it was difficult for a Jew, one of God's chosen people, to realize that God desires to include all humanity in the plan of salvation. Here Paul, the apostle to the Gentiles, gives his rationale for the place of Gentiles in the divine plan of salvation.

A READING FROM THE EPISTLE TO THE ROMANS.

Matthew 15:21–28
This incident is narrowly pro-Jewish. Matthew's point of view was that, before the crucifixion, the gospel was offered to Jews; after the resurrection was the time for preaching to the Gentiles.

A READING FROM THE GOSPEL OF MATTHEW.

Proper 16 (Closest to August 24)

Isaiah 51:1–6
In a poem foretelling the deliverance of the Israelites from their Babylonian exile, God speaks to them through the prophet. God also broadens the thought of deliverance to embrace eternal salvation.

A READING FROM THE BOOK OF ISAIAH.

[*v. 1: Begin* "Thus says the Lord, 'Listen to me. . . .' "]

Romans 11:33–36
This reading is the conclusion of Paul's discussion of the place of Jew and Gentile in the eternal purposes of God. It is a doxological outpouring on God's inscrutable wisdom.

A READING FROM THE EPISTLE TO THE ROMANS.

Matthew 16:13–20
Here Peter puts into words the growing conviction of the disciples as to who Jesus was.

A READING FROM THE GOSPEL OF MATTHEW.

Proper 17 (Closest to August 31)

Jeremiah 15:15–21

Here is probably the occasion when Jeremiah the prophet was unjustly imprisoned in a pit with mud up to his neck. This is his prayer. We get a glimpse of the personality of Jeremiah and of the nature and function of the Hebrew prophet.

A READING FROM THE BOOK OF JEREMIAH.

Romans 12:1–8

This is the beginning of the ethical section of Paul's Epistle to the Romans.

A READING FROM THE EPISTLE TO THE ROMANS.

Matthew 16:21–27

After Peter had put into words the disciples' conviction that Jesus was the Messiah, Jesus begins to broaden their conception of what that meant and of what discipleship meant.

A READING FROM THE GOSPEL OF MATTHEW.

Proper 18 (Closest to September 7)

Ezekiel 33: (1–6) 7–11
Here we see the hard role of the prophet who must proclaim to Israel the will of God, who is both stern and merciful.

A READING FROM THE BOOK OF EZEKIEL.

[*v. 7: Omit* "So"; *begin* "Thus says the Lord God, 'You, mortal, I have made a sentinel. . . .' "]

Romans 12:9–21
In the ethical section of this epistle, Paul deals with our behavior toward others in the church and toward our enemies.

A READING FROM THE EPISTLE TO THE ROMANS.

Matthew 18:15–20
Matthew puts these words into the mouth of Jesus. Perhaps some of them are Jesus' words. But scholars think this is a bit of early church practice in dealing with a community problem.

A READING FROM THE GOSPEL OF MATTHEW.

[*v. 15: Begin* "Jesus said. . . . "]

Proper 19 (Closest to September 14)

Ecclesiasticus 27:30—28:7
This passage is part of the instructions the author of Ecclesiasticus in the Apocrypha includes in his book. It throws considerable light on the forgiveness petition in the Lord's Prayer.

A READING FROM THE BOOK OF ECCLESIASTICUS.

Romans 14:5-12
The closing part of Paul's Epistle to the Romans contains this advice about being sensitive to others' modes of life and ways of expressing their dedication.

A READING FROM THE EPISTLE TO THE ROMANS.

Matthew 18:21-35
While other biblical writers discuss the meaning of forgiveness, Jesus deals with it in a parable.

A READING FROM THE GOSPEL OF MATTHEW.

Proper 20 (Closest to September 21)

Jonah 3:10—4:11

The closing part of the Book of Jonah gives us a humorous contrast between the gracious, forgiving God and the pouting prophet who is upset because God prevented from taking place that prophet's foretelling of doom.

A READING FROM THE BOOK OF JONAH.

[*Begin 3:10* "When God saw what Nineveh did. . . ."]

Philippians 1:21–27

In this reading, Paul, who is in prison, is writing to the church at Philippi. We catch a glimpse of both his inner feelings and his deep pastoral concern.

A READING FROM THE EPISTLE TO THE PHILIPPIANS.

Matthew 20:1–16

It is easy to get angry with God because God does not do what we think is right. God is not answerable to humans. Jesus deals with this in a parable.

A READING FROM THE GOSPEL OF MATTHEW.

[*v. 1: Begin* "Jesus said, . . ."]

Proper 21 (Closest to September 28)

Ezekiel 18:1–4, 25–32
The prophet Ezekiel writes at length about each individual's moral responsibility in the sight of God. This is part of that discourse.

A READING FROM THE BOOK OF EZEKIEL.

Philippians 2:1–13
In Paul's discussion of the Christian life, he has inserted an eloquent and almost lyrical description of the essential meaning of the incarnation. It has been called "the chief glory of the Epistle to the Philippians."

A READING FROM THE EPISTLE TO THE PHILIPPIANS.

Matthew 21:28–32
There is a difference between saying and doing. Jesus discusses it in the Sermon on the Mount. Here he applies it to the religious leaders.

A READING FROM THE GOSPEL OF MATTHEW.

[*v. 28: Begin* "Jesus said. . . ."]

Proper 22 (Closest to October 5)

Isaiah 5:1-7
Here the prophet Isaiah sings a minstrel's song of doom against Israel and Judah because they have failed their vocation as the chosen of the Lord.

A READING FROM THE BOOK OF ISAIAH.

Philippians 3:14-21
This bit of Paul's writing gives us both a glimpse of the apostle's inner life and raises our standards as to what it means to be Christ's faithful servants.

A READING FROM THE EPISTLE TO THE PHILIPPIANS.

Matthew 21:33-43
This allegory is based on a parable of Jesus about Israel, the vineyard of the Lord. It is a story of warning and of judgment.

A READING FROM THE GOSPEL OF MATTHEW.

[v. 33: Begin "Jesus said, 'Listen to another parable. . . .' "]

Proper 23 (Closest to October 12)

Isaiah 25:1-9

This reading is part a poem of thanksgiving for a military victory and part a musing about God's ultimate feast of triumph and the end of all sorrow.

A READING FROM THE BOOK OF ISAIAH.

Philippians 4:4-13

This is the apostle Paul's last communication from prison. Here is dedication and a quietly joyful faith that is the ground of both his inner peace and his treatment of others.

A READING FROM THE EPISTLE TO THE PHILIPPIANS.

Matthew 22:1-14

Here are two early church allegories based on parables of Jesus. One deals with a rationale for evangelizing Gentiles; the other is about repentance as the acceptable garb of one who would stand in the presence of the Lord.

A READING FROM THE GOSPEL OF MATTHEW.

Proper 24 (Closest to October 19)

Isaiah 45:1-7
In this reading, God, speaking through the prophet Isaiah, makes it clear who alone is God and that God uses even the skill and might of Cyrus, king of Persia, to carry out divine purposes.

A READING FROM THE BOOK OF ISAIAH.

1 Thessalonians 1:1-10
Paul begins his Epistle to the Thessalonians with a thanksgiving for the faith of the members of that congregation.

A READING FROM THE FIRST EPISTLE TO THE THESSALONIANS.

Matthew 22:15-22
This is one of a series of Holy Week encounters between the religious authorities and Jesus in which they seek to build up a case against him.

A READING FROM THE GOSPEL OF MATTHEW.

Proper 25 (Closest to October 26)

Exodus 22:21-27

In a section of moral and religious laws are found these verses of compassionate concern for one's neighbor. Out of this concern comes the neighbor commandment quoted by our Lord.

A READING FROM THE BOOK OF EXODUS.

[*v. 21: Begin* "God said to Moses, 'Set these ordinances before the children of Israel: . . . .' "]

1 Thessalonians 2:1-8

Here Paul the apostle gives us a glimpse of the way he probably behaved in every place as he went about the work of spreading the gospel of Jesus Christ.

A READING FROM THE FIRST EPISTLE TO THE THESSALONIANS.

Matthew 22:34-46

In the course of the religious authorities' encounters with Jesus during Holy Week, they asked him the question about the great commandment, which was a matter of continual debate. Jesus' reply put two commandments side by side for perhaps the first time.

A READING FROM THE GOSPEL OF MATTHEW.

[*v. 34: Begin* "When the Pharisees heard that Jesus had silenced. . . ."]

Proper 26 (Closest to November 2)

Micah 3:5–12
The prophet berates the irresponsible leaders of Israel—the prophets who water down their message and the rulers who pervert justice.

A READING FROM THE BOOK OF MICAH.

1 Thessalonians 2:9–13, 17–20
Paul is usually thought of as a great missionary and a profound theologian. Here we sense another side of him: his deep pastoral concern for the people of a church he founded.

A READING FROM THE FIRST EPISTLE TO THE THESSALONIANS.

Matthew 23:1–12
In his Holy Week discourse, Jesus condemns those religious leaders who, through their self-concern, do not practice what they preach and thus lead God's people astray.

A READING FROM THE GOSPEL OF MATTHEW.

[*v. 1: Omit* "Then."]

Proper 27 (Closest to November 9)

Amos 5:18–24

The stern prophet Amos denounces those who are casual about their religious practices and do not take seriously God's demands for justice and right dealings. So they should not anticipate lightly the coming day of the Lord.

A READING FROM THE BOOK OF AMOS.

[*Before v. 21, insert* "Thus says the Lord God."]

1 Thessalonians 4:13–18

Paul and his colleagues believed profoundly in the early return of the Lord. A question had been raised about the state of those believers who had died before Christ's return. This was Paul's answer.

A READING FROM THE FIRST EPISTLE TO THE THESSALONIANS.

Matthew 25:1–13

The parable of the bridesmaids is a warning to the disciples to be prepared and ready to enter the kingdom when the Lord comes. The oil is a symbol of repentance.

A READING FROM THE GOSPEL OF MATTHEW.

[*v. 1: Begin* "Jesus said, 'Then the kingdom. . . .' "]

Proper 28 (Closest to November 16)

Zephaniah 1:7, 12–18

To the prophet Zephaniah, God is uncompromisingly holy, just, and righteous. Hence, the coming day of the Lord will be a time of judgment for those who do not measure up. The Lord's coming is not to be taken lightly.

A READING FROM THE BOOK OF ZEPHANIAH.

1 Thessalonians 5:1–10

In contrast to Old Testament prophets who had an ominous view of the coming day of the Lord, Paul describes his Christian belief about that coming great day.

A READING FROM THE FIRST EPISTLE TO THE THESSALONIANS.

Matthew 25:14–15, 19–29

The parable of the talents is one of Jesus' parables of judgment. We do not wait idly for the day of the Lord's return.

A READING FROM THE GOSPEL OF MATTHEW.

[*v. 14: Begin* "The coming of the kingdom is as if a man, going. . . ."]

70

Proper 29 (Closest to November 23)

Ezekiel 34:11-17
Here God, through the prophet, is described as the Good Shepherd. God exercises more than tender care; God's presence also involves judgment.

A READING FROM THE BOOK OF EZEKIEL.

1 Corinthians 15:20-28
In the chapter in which Paul explains belief in the resurrection from the dead, he makes clear that at the end of time, when history is rolled up, all things will be subjected to God, the eternal Judge.

A READING FROM THE FIRST EPISTLE TO THE CORINTHIANS.

[*v. 20: Begin* "Christ has been raised. . . ." *In v. 28, Read* "When all things are subjected to God. . . ."]

Matthew 25:31-46
This is Jesus' parable of the Last Judgment.

A READING FROM THE GOSPEL OF MATTHEW.

[*v. 31: Begin* "Jesus said. . . ."]

YEAR B

First Sunday of Advent

Isaiah 64:1–9a

The confessional tone of this ancient prayer and its author's deep faith are appropriately ours as the Advent season begins.

A READING FROM THE BOOK OF ISAIAH.

1 Corinthians 1:1–9

The opening paragraph of this epistle of Paul's throws light on the meaning of both being a Christian and of being a member of the church.

A READING FROM THE FIRST EPISTLE TO THE CORINTHIANS.

Mark 13: (24–32) 33–37

The Lord's coming, which we celebrate at Christmas, is twofold: the nativity, a historical event, and his Second Coming, an eschatological event. This Marcan reading is about that Second Coming.

A READING FROM THE GOSPEL OF MARK.

Second Sunday of Advent

Isaiah 40:1–11

This poem could be entitled "The Coming of the Lord." Historically, the occasion was probably the end of the Babylonian exile, but these words are associated in our minds with John the Baptist and the coming of Jesus.

A READING FROM THE BOOK OF ISAIAH.

2 Peter 3:8–15a, 18

The second-century Christian church thought that the Second Coming of Christ, the righteous Judge, was very near. We may not share their view, but Advent causes us to consider seriously, as did they, the sort of lives of holiness and godliness we should be leading.

A READING FROM THE SECOND EPISTLE OF PETER.

Mark 1:1–8

John the Baptist heralded the coming of Christ as Scripture foretold. This is Mark's brief account of John's ministry.

A READING FROM THE GOSPEL OF MARK.

Third Sunday of Advent

Isaiah 65:17–25

In this reading, God is speaking through the prophet about the final day of the Lord. The Christian associates all this with the Second Coming of Christ.

A READING FROM THE BOOK OF ISAIAH.

[v. 17: Begin "Thus says the Lord."]

1 Thessalonians 5:(12–15) 16–28

With these words, Paul closes his first letter to the Christians at Thessalonica. It is evident that those early Christians lived in tiptoe expectancy of the imminent return of their Lord. Their attitude is that to which we aspire as we prepare for Christmas.

A READING FROM THE FIRST EPISTLE TO THE THESSALONIANS.

John 1:6–8, 19–28, or John 3:23–30

John the Baptist is only of interest to gospel writers as the forerunner of Jesus and as the one who prepared people for Jesus' coming. This is one of two such references in the Fourth Gospel.

A READING FROM THE GOSPEL OF JOHN.

Fourth Sunday of Advent

2 Samuel 7:4, 8–16

Through Nathan the prophet, God tells King David what his destiny shall be. Generations later, Jesus was known as the Son of David.

A READING FROM THE SECOND BOOK OF SAMUEL.

[*v. 4: Read only* "The word of the Lord came to Nathan: Go and tell my servant David." *Begin v. 8* "Thus says the Lord. . . ."]

Romans 16:25–27

This is the ascription with which the Epistle to the Romans closes. It embodies what we joyfully carol at Christmastime.

A READING FROM THE EPISTLE TO THE ROMANS.

Luke 1:26–38

This eve-of-Christmas gospel reading is the angel's announcement to Mary.

A READING FROM THE GOSPEL OF LUKE.

Christmas Day I

Isaiah 9:2–4, 6–7

The prophet wrote this poem about the Messiah who was to come. You decide how accurately he foresees the role Jesus was to fill.

A READING FROM THE BOOK OF ISAIAH.

Titus 2:11–14

This epistle was perhaps read in church to Christians living about a century after the crucifixion-resurrection.

A READING FROM THE EPISTLE TO TITUS.

Luke 2:1–14 (15–20)

THE NATIVITY STORY ACCORDING TO LUKE.

Christmas Day II

Isaiah 62:6–7, 10–12
Here are two stanzas of a poem describing the chosen people of God. The second pictures that people when the Messiah comes.

A READING FROM THE BOOK OF ISAIAH.

Titus 3:4–7
This advice to early Christian leaders becomes an appropriate sermonette when we hear it on this day.

A READING FROM THE EPISTLE TO TITUS.

[*vs. 4: Omit* "But."]

Luke 2:(1–14) 15–20
Our whole biblical memory of Christmas centers in the angelic announcement to the shepherds and their visit to the Christ Child.

A READING FROM THE GOSPEL OF LUKE.

Christmas Day III

Isaiah 52:7-10

Here are stanzas from a poem that might be entitled, "The Lord Has Become King." They are of a piece with our celebration of the birth of Christ the Savior.

A READING FROM THE BOOK OF ISAIAH.

Hebrews 1:1-12

This epistle opens with a description of the incarnation of God's Son in terms of its eternal significance.

A READING FROM THE EPISTLE TO THE HEBREWS.

John 1:1-14

The Fourth Gospel opens with a description of the eternal significance of the coming of God's Son and people's response to that coming. The meaning of "the Word" is pivotal. It embraces God's creative power, purpose, and wisdom.

A READING FROM THE GOSPEL OF JOHN.

First Sunday after Christmas

Isaiah 61:10—62:3

In this poem, an ancient seer sings of the glad tidings of salvation to Zion. Heard on this day, these words become part of the profound joy of the feast of Christ's nativity.

A READING FROM THE BOOK OF ISAIAH.

Galatians 3:23-25; 4:4-7

With the coming of Christ, our relation to God has changed from legalism to faith. The apostle explains what this change means.

A READING FROM THE EPISTLE TO THE GALATIANS.

[*Because verses have been skipped, change* "But" *to* "For" *in 4:4.*]

John 1:1-18

The prologue of the Fourth Gospel explains the eternal significance of the coming of God's Son and of the new relationship with God that results from that coming. The word *grace* means undeserved, unexpected kindness and caring.

A READING FROM THE GOSPEL OF JOHN.

Holy Name (January 1)

Exodus 34:1–8

When Moses had received the Ten Commandments from God on Mount Sinai, he went down, only to find the children of Israel worshiping a golden calf. In his anger, he broke the tablets on which the commandments were written. Now Moses goes up the mountain a second time to receive the commandments from God.

A READING FROM THE BOOK OF EXODUS.

Romans 1:1–7

In the salutation with which his epistle opens, Paul tells what motivated him to become a Christian evangelist.

A READING FROM THE EPISTLE TO THE ROMANS.

Luke 2:15–21

This part of the nativity story includes the account of the Jewish ceremony in which the baby Jesus received his name.

A READING FROM THE GOSPEL OF LUKE.

Second Sunday after Christmas

Jeremiah 31:7–14
This is a poem about the return to Zion of exiles from all nations.

A READING FROM THE BOOK OF JEREMIAH.

Ephesians 1:3–6, 15–19a
The Epistle to the Ephesians opens with this thanksgiving, which describes what the coming of Jesus Christ is intended to mean in our lives.

A READING FROM THE FIRST EPISTLE TO THE EPHESIANS.

Matthew 2:13–15, 19–23
This is the account of the flight of the Holy Family into Egypt.

A READING FROM THE GOSPEL OF MATTHEW.

[*v. 13: Substitute* "the Wise Men" *for* "they."]

or Luke 2:41–52
This is the only story of Jesus' childhood in the gospels.

A READING FROM THE GOSPEL OF LUKE.

[*v. 41: Substitute* "Jesus" *for* "his."]

or Matthew 2:1–12
This is the account of the Wise Men coming to worship the Christ Child.

A READING FROM THE GOSPEL OF MATTHEW.

The Epiphany (January 6)

Isaiah 60:1–6, 9
The prophet gives this message of hope to the Babylonian exiles. It seems to put into poetry the message of the story of the Wise Men.

A READING FROM THE BOOK OF ISAIAH.

Ephesians 3:1–12
It was shocking to Jewish Christians that Gentiles were on an equal footing with them in the Christian church. That radical truth is the theme of this epistle.

A READING FROM THE EPISTLE TO THE EPHESIANS.

[v. 1: Omit "This is the reason that."]

Matthew 2:1–12
The story of the Wise Men sets forth the Epiphany message in picture pageantry.

A READING FROM THE GOSPEL OF MATTHEW.

First Sunday after Epiphany

Isaiah 42:1–9

This ancient poem describes the servant of the Lord. Christians have always thought of Jesus Christ as fulfilling that role.

A READING FROM THE BOOK OF ISAIAH.

[*v. 1: Begin* "Thus says the Lord. . . ."]

Acts 10:34–38

Paul addresses the Roman centurion Cornelius and his family, who were eager to be baptized. This was a breakthrough occasion: Gentiles becoming Christians quite apart from the restrictions of Judaism.

A READING FROM THE BOOK OF ACTS.

Mark 1:7–11

This is Mark's account of the baptism of Jesus.

A READING FROM THE GOSPEL OF MARK.

[*v. 7: Read* "John the Baptist proclaimed. . . ."]

Second Sunday after Epiphany

1 Samuel 3:1–10 (11–20)

Young Samuel was the houseboy of Eli, the high priest, and had responsibilities in the temple at Shiloh. This is the story of how God called him to be the prophet who ushered in a new day in the life of the people of Israel.

A READING FROM THE FIRST BOOK OF SAMUEL.

1 Corinthians 6:11b–20

In this reading, the apostle is speaking to a problem in the church of another day. Yet when heard in a culture of drugs and alcohol, of physical exercise and dieting, his words are still relevant.

A READING FROM THE FIRST EPISTLE TO THE CORINTHIANS.

[*v. 11b: Omit* "But."]

John 1:43–51

The Lord calls Philip and Nathaniel to be his disciples.

A READING FROM THE GOSPEL OF JOHN.

Third Sunday after Epiphany

Jeremiah 3:21—4:2

Early in his ministry, the prophet Jeremiah issued this call to genuine repentance.

A READING FROM THE BOOK OF JEREMIAH.

[*Before v. 22, add* "The Lord said to them. . . ." *Before v. 22b, add* "And the people of Israel replied. . . ."]

1 Corinthians 7:17–23

In a section of his epistle filled with advice to fellow Christians, the apostle makes clear that one's status in the world is not of primary importance so far as being a servant of the Lord is concerned, and he tells what is important.

A READING FROM THE FIRST EPISTLE TO THE CORINTHIANS.

[*v. 17: Begin* "Let each of you. . . ."]

Mark 1:14–20

Here is a glimpse of the very beginning of Jesus' ministry.

A READING FROM THE GOSPEL OF MARK.

Fourth Sunday after Epiphany

Deuteronomy 18:15–20
This reading is the only place in the Bible where prophecy is described as an institution, and here also a genuine prophet is described.

A READING FROM THE BOOK OF DEUTERONOMY.

[*v. 15: Begin* "Moses summoned all Israel and said to them. . . ."]

1 Corinthians 8:1b–13
In this reading, Paul is dealing with a religious problem of first-century Christians: eating food that had been offered to idols. The principle he enunciates throws revealing light on the observance of the Golden Rule.

A READING FROM THE FIRST EPISTLE TO THE CORINTHIANS.

[*The point of the passage will be clearer if you omit vv. 5–9. Then begin v. 10* "But if others see. . . ."]

Mark 1:21–28
As Jesus' ministry of teaching and healing begins, notice the way both the evil spirits and the people react to his authority.

A READING FROM THE GOSPEL OF MARK.

[*v. 21: Begin* "Jesus and his disciples went. . . ."]

Fifth Sunday after Epiphany

2 Kings 4:(8–17) 18–21 (22–31) 32–37

This is one of the wonder stories in the saga of Elisha the prophet. Whatever may be the facts, people remembered him as a man of God, and many wonderful happenings are associated with his name.

A READING FROM THE BOOK OF KINGS.

[If the entire passage (4:8–37) is not to be read, perhaps the most intelligible edited version is 4:8–21, 32–37.]

1 Corinthians 9:16–23

In this reading, Paul the apostle gives an autobiographical glimpse of himself. He is driven by a divine compulsion to preach the gospel, and he tells how he tries to do this most effectively.

A READING FROM THE FIRST EPISTLE TO THE CORINTHIANS.

Mark 1:29–39

Here is a description of what may have been a typical twenty-four-hour period in Jesus' early ministry.

A READING FROM THE GOSPEL OF MARK.

[v. 29: Read "As soon as Jesus and his disciples left the synagogue. . . ."*]*

Sixth Sunday after Epiphany

2 Kings 5:1–15ab

The healing of Naaman the leper is part of the saga of Elisha, the man of God.

A READING FROM THE SECOND BOOK OF KINGS.

[*v. 15: Conclude with the words* "no God in all the earth except in Israel."]

1 Corinthians 9:24–27

The apostle concludes a longer section on the Christian's freedom with this advice on self-discipline.

A READING FROM THE FIRST EPISTLE TO THE CORINTHIANS.

Mark 1:40–45

This is one of many times that Jesus reveals the power of God to save.

A READING FROM THE GOSPEL OF MARK.

Seventh Sunday after Epiphany

Isaiah 43:18–25

Throughout the poetry of Second Isaiah runs the conviction that God, the Holy One of Israel, genuinely cares for the chosen people. These verses illustrate this.

A READING FROM THE BOOK OF ISAIAH.

[*v. 18: Begin* "Thus says the Lord. . . ."]

2 Corinthians 1:18–22

The apostle is here explaining his conviction that God can be depended upon. The Lord does not vacillate in concern for us.

A READING FROM THE SECOND EPISTLE TO THE CORINTHIANS.

Mark 2:1–12

In the time of Jesus, affliction was considered to be evidence of sin. Hence, the act of healing and divine forgiveness were thought of as the same. Such was the mind-set of the people on this occasion.

A READING FROM THE GOSPEL OF MARK.

[*v. 1: Read* "When Jesus returned. . . ."]

Eighth Sunday after Epiphany

Hosea 2:14–23
Because of Israel's apostasy, God, through the prophet, speaks of that nation as God's unfaithful bride whom, in compassion, the Lord intends to woo back.

A READING FROM THE BOOK OF HOSEA.

[*v. 14: Read* "Thus says the Lord, 'Behold, I will allure Israel, my bride, and bring her. . . .' "]

2 Corinthians 3:(4–11) 17—4:2
The apostle explains what knowing the Lord through the presence of God's Spirit means in the life of a Christian.

A READING FROM THE SECOND EPISTLE TO THE CORINTHIANS.

Mark 2:18–22
Being with Jesus turned the disciples' lives around. Their behavior—as well as his words and deeds—was the cause of the opposition to Jesus.

A READING FROM THE GOSPEL OF MARK.

[*v. 18: Substitute* "Jesus" *for* "him."]

Last Sunday after Epiphany

1 Kings 19:9–18

Elijah, the beleagued, lonely prophet, has fled Queen Jezebel's wrath, and God appears to him at his mountain hideaway. This is what happened.

A READING FROM THE FIRST BOOK OF KINGS.

[*v. 9: Begin* "On Horeb, the mount of God, Elijah came to a cave. . . ." *Omit v. 17.*]

2 Peter 1:16–19 (20–21)

The transfiguration of Jesus is told in each of the first three gospels and here in this epistle, whose author was with Jesus on that occasion.

A READING FROM THE SECOND EPISTLE OF PETER.

Mark 9:2–9

On the Mount of Transfiguration, the disciples' vision made clear that Jesus fulfilled their ancient religious tradition.

A READING FROM THE GOSPEL OF MARK.

[*v. 2: Read* "Six days after Peter had first put into words the disciples' growing conviction that Jesus was the Messiah, Jesus took with him. . . ."]

Ash Wednesday

Joel 2:1–2, 12–17
In about 400 B.C. the prophet Joel sees in a locust plague the ultimate judgment of God, the day of the Lord. His call to repent is appropriately ours on Ash Wednesday.

A READING FROM THE BOOK OF JOEL.

or Isaiah 58:1–12
God, through an unknown ancient prophet, berates his people because their worship does not result in just and righteous behavior. His message is appropriate to our thinking as we enter the season of Lent.

A READING FROM THE BOOK OF ISAIAH.

[*v. 1: Begin,* "Thus says the Lord."]

2 Corinthians 5:20–6:10
Paul, using himself as an example, explains to Corinthian Christians the discipline of life and the endurance of suffering which being a follower of Christ entails.

A READING FROM THE SECOND EPISTLE TO THE CORINTHIANS.

[*v. 20: Omit* "So."]

Matthew 6:1–6, 16–21
In the Sermon on the Mount, Jesus teaches his followers the way in which their practice of piety will be acceptable to God.

A READING FROM THE GOSPEL OF MATTHEW.

[*v. 1: Begin,* "Jesus said."]

First Sunday in Lent

Genesis 9:8–17

A foundation stone of biblical religion is God's covenant with Israel. God saves Noah from the Flood waters, and the rainbow is the sign of the covenant between this saving God and the chosen people.

A READING FROM THE BOOK OF GENESIS.

[v. 8: Omit "Then."]

1 Peter 3:18–22

In this early Christian epistle, Peter contrasts the baptism of believers in Christ's resurrection with what took place in the Noah-and-the-Flood saga.

A READING FROM THE FIRST EPISTLE OF PETER.

[v. 18: Omit "For."]

Mark 1:9–13

This is Mark's description of Jesus' baptism and his terse account of the Lord's temptations in the wilderness.

A READING FROM THE GOSPEL OF MARK.

Second Sunday in Lent

Genesis 22:1–14

This is one of the stories in the Abraham saga. Abraham is known as the father of the faithful as much for this incident as for any other.

A READING FROM THE BOOK OF GENESIS.

[v. 1: Omit "After these things."]

Romans 8:31–39

Just as Abraham's faith is a major part of our religious heritage, so also is Paul's great faith that nothing can separate us from the love of Christ.

A READING FROM THE EPISTLE TO THE ROMANS.

[v. 31: Omit the first sentence; begin "If God is for us. . . ."]

Mark 8:31–38

Jesus and his disciples are enroute to Jerusalem for the last time. This is part of his revolutionary teaching regarding the role of the Messiah and of those who would follow him.

A READING FROM THE GOSPEL OF MARK.

[v. 31: Omit "Then."]

Third Sunday in Lent

Exodus 20:1–17

The Ten Commandments.

A READING FROM THE BOOK OF EXODUS.

[*v. 1: Omit "Then."*]

Romans 7:13–25

This reading is the apostle Paul's psycho-logical analysis of the entrapping nature of sin and of the only way of escape.

A READING FROM THE EPISTLE TO THE ROMANS.

John 2:13–22

Jesus momentarily destroys the trading that went on in the outer court of the Temple, symbolic of overthrowing the old religious system and replacing it with allegiance to himself.

A READING FROM THE GOSPEL OF JOHN.

Fourth Sunday in Lent

2 Chronicles 36:14–23

The Hebrews believed that God controls the events of history. This summary at the end of the Book of Chronicles makes that conviction clear.

A READING FROM THE SECOND BOOK OF CHRONICLES.

[*v. 14: Begin* "During the reign of Zedekiah in Jerusalem, the king, all the leading priests. . . ."]

Ephesians 2:4–10

The author of this epistle is explaining the nature of Christian salvation.

A READING FROM THE EPISTLE TO THE EPHESIANS.

[*v. 4: Omit* "But."]

John 6:4–15

This is John's account of the feeding of the five thousand.

A READING FROM THE GOSPEL OF JOHN.

Fifth Sunday in Lent

Jeremiah 31:31–34

This reading is the high point of Old Testament prophetic insight. It influenced the thinking of Paul in his epistles and is quoted twice in the Epistle to the Hebrews.

A READING FROM THE BOOK OF JEREMIAH.

Hebrews 5: (1–4) 5–10

The new covenant with God described by the prophet Jeremiah is possible not because of our good works but because of the high priesthood of Jesus Christ. Here is how he acquired that role.

A READING FROM THE EPISTLE TO THE HEBREWS.

[*v. 5: Omit* "So also."]

John 12:20–33

The coming of certain Greeks to worship Jesus is a foretaste of what will be after his death and resurrection. Then all people will be drawn to the worship of God.

A READING FROM THE GOSPEL OF JOHN.

Palm Sunday

Mark 11:1–11a
Here is the account of the occasion from which Palm Sunday takes its name.

A READING FROM THE GOSPEL OF MARK.

[*v. 1: Substitute* "Jesus" *for* "he." *End v. 11a with* "went into the temple."]

Isaiah 45:21–25
These verses are part of a poem in which God speaks through the prophet concerning the conversion of the nations.

A READING FROM THE BOOK OF ISAIAH.

[*v. 21: Begin* "Thus says the Lord."]

or Isaiah 52:13—53:12
This suffering servant poem is one of the spiritual high points of the Old Testament. It is a remarkable description of the meaning of Christ's passion, which was to take place centuries later.

A READING FROM THE BOOK OF ISAIAH.

Philippians 2:5–11
Here in a nutshell is Paul's belief about Jesus Christ.

A READING FROM THE EPISTLE TO THE PHILIPPIANS.

Mark (14:32–72) 15:1–39 (40–47)
The passion and death of Jesus Christ according to Mark.

A READING FROM THE GOSPEL OF MARK.

Maundy Thursday

Exodus 12:1–14a
This is the origin of the Feast of the Passover, the symbolism of which lies behind the Lord's Supper.

A READING FROM THE BOOK OF EXODUS.

1 Corinthians 11:23–26 (27–32)
This is the earliest account of the institution of the Lord's Supper. Paul wrote to the Corinthian Christians almost two decades before the first gospel appeared.

A READING FROM THE FIRST EPISTLE TO THE CORINTHIANS.

John 13:1–15
This is the only account of the Last Supper in John's Gospel. Earlier, following the feeding of the five thousand, Jesus discusses what it means to "eat the flesh of the Son of Man and to drink his blood."

A READING FROM THE GOSPEL OF JOHN.

or Luke 22:14–30
This is Luke's account of the institution of the Lord's Supper.

A READING FROM THE GOSPEL OF LUKE.

[v. 14 Read, "When the hour had come, Jesus took his place. . . ."]

Good Friday

Isaiah 52:13—53:12
This is the best known of the servant of the Lord poems in Isaiah. Its deep spiritual insights have lead the Church to describe the Lord's passion in its phrases.

A READING FROM THE BOOK OF ISAIAH.

or Genesis 22:1–18
The story of Abraham's willingness to sacrifice his son at God's command without losing faith in the goodness of God's eternal purposes, adds a dimension of meaning to the Lord's passion.

A READING FROM THE BOOK OF GENESIS.

[v. 1: Omit "After these things."]

or Wisdom 2:1, 12–24
This passage sounds like an elaboration of the thoughts of the high priest and his colleagues who were responsible for the Lord's passion and death.

A READING FROM THE BOOK OF WISDOM.

Hebrews 10:1–25
Here a New Testament writer seeks to explain the significance of the fact that the blood of Jesus was shed for us.

A READING FROM THE EPISTLE TO THE HEBREWS.

John (18:1–40); 19:1–37
The passion of our Lord Jesus Christ according to John.

Easter Day

Acts 10:34–43
Here is part of an early Christian sermon preached by Peter, the leading disciple, who was one of the first to see the risen Lord.

A READING FROM THE BOOK OF ACTS.

[*v. 34: Omit,* "Then."]

or Isaiah 25:6–9
This little prophetic passage foretells God's ultimate victory: the feast of triumph and the end of sorrow.

A READING FROM THE BOOK OF ISAIAH.

Colossians 3:1–4
Here Paul describes the difference belief in the resurrection of Christ is intended to make in the life of every believer.

A READING FROM THE EPISTLE TO THE COLOSSIANS.

Mark 16:1–8
This is Mark's account of what happened on the first Easter morning.

A READING FROM THE GOSPEL OF MARK.

Easter Evening

Acts 5:29a, 30–32

Peter and the other apostles had defied the religious authorities by preaching that Jesus had risen from the dead. They were arrested and brought before the Sanhedrin. This was Peter's defense.

A READING FROM THE BOOK OF ACTS.

[*v. 29: Omit* "But."]

or Daniel 12:1–3

This vision from the Book of Daniel is the first clear mention in the Old Testament of a resurrection of the wicked as well as the righteous.

A READING FROM THE BOOK OF DANIEL.

1 Corinthians 5:6b–8

In the Passover ritual, unleavened bread was associated with the remembrance of Israel's redemption from Egypt—a people's new start. Here Paul transfers that ancient association to Christ's resurrection and the new start that is ours because of the risen Christ.

A READING FROM THE FIRST EPISTLE TO THE CORINTHIANS.

Luke 24:13–35

Luke's Easter evening account is significant because the ways those disciples knew the risen Lord are ours also.

A READING FROM THE GOSPEL OF LUKE.

[*v. 13: Begin* "Now on that same day, two of Jesus' followers were going. . . ."]

Second Sunday of Easter

Acts 3:12a, 13–15, 17–26
As Peter and John were entering the Temple, they were accosted by a lame beggar. Instead of giving him alms, Peter healed him. A crowd quickly gathered. This is what happened next.

A READING FROM THE BOOK OF ACTS.

[*v. 12a: Read* "When Peter saw that a crowd was gathering because of the lame man he had healed, he addressed the people." *This reediting of the account is recommended: Acts 3:12–15, 17–21, 25–26.*]

or Isaiah 26:2–9, 19
This eighth-century B.C. song of thanksgiving for victory brings to mind our joy over the Lord's victorious resurrection.

A READING FROM THE BOOK OF ISAIAH.

1 John 5:1–6
In this epistle reading, the writer explains what it means to have faith in Christ the risen Lord.

A READING FROM THE FIRST EPISTLE OF JOHN.

John 20:19–31
This is John's account of what took place on the evening of the first Easter Day.

A READING FROM THE GOSPEL OF JOHN.

Third Sunday of Easter

Acts 4:5–12

When Peter and John were entering the Temple, they were accosted at the gate by a lame beggar seeking alms. Instead of giving alms, Peter healed him. In the excitement that followed, the apostles were arrested. This was Peter's defense when they were brought before the Sanhedrin.

A READING FROM THE BOOK OF ACTS.

or Micah 4:1–5

Here is the prophet's vision of a glorious time to come. Believers in the Lord's resurrection can share his enthusiasm.

A READING FROM THE BOOK OF MICAH.

1 John 1:1—2:2

The author of this epistle, written near the end of the first century, speaks with authority based on his awareness of the presence of the risen Christ.

A READING FROM THE FIRST EPISTLE OF JOHN.

Luke 24:36b–48

Luke's gospel closes with this account of the Lord's final resurrection appearance.

A READING FROM THE GOSPEL OF LUKE.

[v. 36: Begin "Jesus himself stood. . . ."]

Fourth Sunday of Easter

Acts 4:(23–31) 32–37

Here is a vignette of life in the company of Christian believers less than a generation after the crucifixion-resurrection.

A READING FROM THE BOOK OF ACTS.

[*v. 23: Read* "After Peter and John were released. . . ."]

or Ezekiel 34:1–10

Here the prophet condemns the leaders of Israel for their lack of a shepherdlike concern for the welfare of God's people.

A READING FROM THE BOOK OF EZEKIEL.

1 John 3:1–8

This epistle was written near the end of the first century. In it, the writer contrasts the characteristics of the children of God and the children of the evil one.

A READING FROM THE FIRST EPISTLE OF JOHN.

John 10:11–16

This is a part of Jesus' description of himself as "the Good Shepherd."

A READING FROM THE GOSPEL OF JOHN.

[*v. 11: Begin* "Jesus said, 'I am. . . .' "]

Fifth Sunday of Easter

Acts 8:26–40

This vignette from the life of the early church —perhaps not more than five years after the crucifixion-resurrection—shows that the Lord's commission, "Go . . . make disciples of all nations, baptizing them . . ." was being obeyed.

A READING FROM THE BOOK OF ACTS.

[v. 26: Omit "Then."]

or Deuteronomy 4:32–40

This is Moses' basic reason why the Israelites should keep God's commandments. It also applies to us.

A READING FROM THE BOOK OF DEUTERONOMY.

[v. 32: Begin "Moses addressed the children of Israel saying. . . ."]

1 John 3:(14–17) 18–24

In this part of his epistle, John adds details to the meaning of the Lord's "new commandment . . . that you love one another."

A READING FROM THE FIRST EPISTLE OF JOHN.

John 14:15–21

In his upper room discourse before his passion, Jesus helps his followers understand what loving him means.

A READING FROM THE GOSPEL OF JOHN.

[v. 15: Begin "Jesus said to them. . . ."]

Sixth Sunday of Easter (Rogation Sunday)

Acts 11:19–30

At the beginning of the Christian era, the believers to whom the risen Christ appeared all happened to be Jews. It was a decade or so before Christianity began to break out of the mold of an all-Jewish religion. Here is a bit of that early breakthrough.

A READING FROM THE BOOK OF ACTS.

or Isaiah 45:11–13, 18–19

Here are stanzas from a prophet's poem that make it clear the Creator has a deep concern for the natural world.

A READING FROM THE BOOK OF ISAIAH.

1 John 4:7–21

This reading deals with the implications of the Christian imperative "Love one another."

A READING FROM THE FIRST EPISTLE OF JOHN.

John 15:9–17

In this part of the Lord's upper room discourse, he discusses "Love one another."

A READING FROM THE GOSPEL OF JOHN.

[*v. 9: Begin* "Jesus said to them. . . ."]

Ascension Day

Acts 1:1-11
Luke begins his Book of Acts with this description of Jesus' last resurrection appearance.

A READING FROM THE BOOK OF ACTS.

or Ezekiel 1:3-5a, 15-22, 26-28
This ancient prophet had a vision of heaven. It is both inscrutable and awesome which is perhaps true of every human vision of heaven.

A READING FROM THE BOOK OF EZEKIEL.

Ephesians 1:15-23
The author of this epistle explains the significance of Christ's ascension to the Christians in Ephesus.

A READING FROM THE EPISTLE TO THE EPHESIANS.

Luke 24:49-53
Luke describes the Lord's ascension, his last resurrection appearance, twice—here at the end of his gospel and in the opening chapter of Acts. The promise of "power from on high"—the Lord's Spirit and continual presence—makes this an occasion of great joy.

A READING FROM THE GOSPEL OF LUKE.

[*v. 49: Omit* "And."]

or Mark 16:9-15, 19-20
This is Mark's account of the Lord's resurrection appearances and of his ascension.

A READING FROM THE GOSPEL OF MARK.

[*v. 9: Read,* "Now after Jesus rose on the first day. . . ."]

Seventh Sunday of Easter

Acts 1:15–26
Here is Luke's account of what took place during the ten days between the Lord's ascension into heaven and the coming of the Holy Spirit on the Day of Pentecost.

A READING FROM THE BOOK OF ACTS.

or Exodus 28:1–4, 9–10, 29–30
This is a description of the ancient beginning of the high priesthood in the traditions of Israel.

A READING FROM THE BOOK OF EXODUS.

[*v. 1: Begin* "God said to Moses, 'Bring near to you. . . .' "]

1 John 5:9–15
In the closing chapter of John's first epistle, the author drives home the importance of that which has been the theme of his whole epistle.

A READING FROM THE FIRST EPISTLE OF JOHN.

John 17:11b–19
This is part of the high priestly prayer of Jesus for his disciples shortly before his passion. Here he is interceding for them, an activity germane to the role of high priest.

A READING FROM THE GOSPEL OF JOHN.

[*v. 11b: Begin* "Jesus prayed, 'Holy Father. . . .' "]

Day of Pentecost

Acts 2:1–11
The first Christian Pentecost occurred on the ancient Jewish feast of that name, fifty days after that Feast of the Passover during which the crucifixion had taken place. This is what happened that has made Pentecost such an important Christian festival.

A READING FROM THE BOOK OF ACTS.

or Isaiah 44:1–8
This sixth-century B.C. poem about what God is doing for God's people sounds like a fore-telling of what took place on the first Christian Pentecost.

A READING FROM THE BOOK OF ISAIAH.

1 Corinthians 12:4–13
On Pentecost, the Holy Spirit first came upon Christian believers in the risen Lord. Here are some of the ways the presence of the Spirit has since manifested itself in the lives of Christians.

A READING FROM THE FIRST EPISTLE TO THE CORINTHIANS.

John 20:19–23
This is John's account of when the disciples first received the Holy Spirit.

A READING FROM THE GOSPEL OF JOHN.

[v. 19: Begin "On the evening of that first Easter day. . . ."]

or John 14:8–17
In his upper room discourse, Jesus tells the disciples about the Holy Spirit they shall shortly receive.

A READING FROM THE GOSPEL OF JOHN.

Trinity Sunday

Exodus 3:1–6

Here Moses comes into God's presence in a most unlikely place.

A READING FROM THE BOOK OF EXODUS.

Romans 8:12–17

In this reading, Paul identifies the Spirit of God both with the Father and with Christ. This line of thought led in time to the Christian doctrine of the Trinity.

A READING FROM THE EPISTLE TO THE ROMANS.

John 3:1–16

The account of Nicodemus's visit to Jesus contains the elements of what later became the doctrine of the Trinity.

A READING FROM THE GOSPEL OF JOHN.

Proper 1 (Closest to May 11)

2 Kings 5:1–15ab

The healing of Naaman the leper is part of the saga of Elisha, the man of God.

A READING FROM THE SECOND BOOK OF KINGS.

[*v. 15: Conclude with the words* "no God in all the earth except in Israel."]

1 Corinthians 9:24–27

The apostle concludes a longer section on the Christian's freedom with this advice on self-discipline.

A READING FROM THE FIRST EPISTLE TO THE CORINTHIANS.

Mark 1:40–45

This is one of many times that Jesus reveals the power of God to save.

A READING FROM THE GOSPEL OF MARK.

[*v. 40: Read* "A leper came to Jesus. . . ."]

Proper 2 (Closest to May 18)

Isaiah 43:18–25
Throughout the poetry of Second Isaiah runs the conviction that God, the Holy One of Israel, genuinely cares for the chosen people. These verses illustrate this.

A READING FROM THE BOOK OF ISAIAH.

[*v. 18: Begin* "Thus says the Lord. . . ."]

2 Corinthians 1:18–22
The apostle is here explaining his conviction that God can be depended upon. The Lord does not vacillate in his concern for us.

A READING FROM THE SECOND EPISTLE TO THE CORINTHIANS.

Mark 2:1–12
In the time of Jesus, affliction was considered to be evidence of sin. Hence, the act of healing and divine forgiveness were thought of as the same. Such was the mind-set of the people on this occasion.

A READING FROM THE GOSPEL OF MARK.

[*v. 1: Read* "When Jesus returned. . . ."]

Proper 3 (Closest to May 25)

Hosea 2:14–23

Because of Israel's apostasy, God, through the prophet, speaks of that nation as God's unfaithful bride whom, in compassion, the Lord intends to woo back.

A READING FROM THE BOOK OF HOSEA.

[*v. 14: Read* "Thus says the Lord, 'I will allure Israel, my bride, and bring her. . . .' "]

2 Corinthians 3:(4–11) 17–4:2

The apostle explains what knowing the Lord through the presence of God's Spirit means in the life of a Christian.

A READING FROM THE SECOND EPISTLE TO THE CORINTHIANS.

Mark 2:18–22

Being with Jesus turned the disciples' lives around. Their behavior—as well as his words and deeds—was the cause of the opposition to Jesus.

A READING FROM THE GOSPEL OF MARK.

[*v. 18: Substitute* "Jesus" *for* "him."]

Proper 4 (Closest to June 1)

Deuteronomy 5:6–21

The Ten Commandments.

A READING FROM THE BOOK OF DEUTERONOMY.

[*v. 6: Begin* "Moses convened all Israel and said to them, 'Hear, O Israel, the statutes and ordinances of the Lord our God. He said, "I am the Lord." ' "]

2 Corinthians 4:5–12

Here Paul gives us a biographical glimpse both of his conviction about Jesus Christ and of what it has cost him to proclaim it.

A READING FROM THE SECOND EPISTLE TO THE CORINTHIANS.

Mark 2:23–28

Jesus and the religious leaders differed in their attitudes toward God's law. The opposition we see here ultimately brought him to the cross.

A READING FROM THE GOSPEL OF MARK.

[*v. 23: Begin* "One sabbath day Jesus was going. . . ."]

Proper 5 (Closest to June 8)

Genesis 3:(1–7) 8–21

Here is eternal truth conveyed in a story. It describes the nature of human sin. Both God's punishment and caring are also described.

A READING FROM THE BOOK OF GENESIS.

[*v. 8: Begin* "Adam and Eve heard the sound. . . ."]

2 Corinthians 4:13–18

In this reading, the apostle reassures those whose lives are in difficult circumstances of the overarching grace of God.

A READING FROM THE SECOND EPISTLE TO THE CORINTHIANS.

Mark 3:20–35

Here is teaching from the early months of Jesus' ministry and evidence of his growing popularity.

A READING FROM THE GOSPEL OF MARK.

[*v. 20: Begin* "The crowd came together again so that Jesus and his disciples could not. . . ."]

Proper 6 (Closest to June 15)

Ezekiel 31:1–6, 10–14

The prophet pronounces doom on the glory and vaunted pride of Egypt. God is the judge of the nations and the ruler of history; both people and nations should live accordingly.

A READING FROM THE BOOK OF EZEKIEL.

[*vv. 10–12: Read* "you" *and* "your" *instead of* "it" *and* "its."]

2 Corinthians 5:1–10

Here the apostle speaks with assurance built on faith about his belief in the hereafter.

A READING FROM THE SECOND EPISTLE TO THE CORINTHIANS.

[*If vv. 2, 3, and 4 are omitted, the point of the passage will be clearer to the congregation.*]

Mark 4:26-34

Here are two of Jesus' parables that throw light on how the kingdom of God will come.

A READING FROM THE GOSPEL OF MARK.

[*v. 26: Begin* "Jesus said . . . ."]

Proper 7 (Closest to June 22)

Job 38:1–11, 16–18

In the drama of Job, after his friends have ceased giving advice and Job has spun out the extent of his anguish of soul and his frustration, God finally speaks. We catch an awesome glimpse of the Creator almost in the act of creating.

A READING FROM THE BOOK OF JOB.

2 Corinthians 5:14–21

The apostle explains what God in Christ has done for us and how we are to respond.

A READING FROM THE SECOND EPISTLE TO THE CORINTHIANS.

Mark 4:35–41 (5:1–20)

The disciples called Jesus "Lord." Here they discover that his authority is greater than they had imagined.

A READING FROM THE GOSPEL OF MARK.

[v. 35: Begin "On that day when evening had come, Jesus said to the disciples. . . ."]

Proper 8 (Closest to June 29)

Deuteronomy 15:7–11

In his discussion of the Year of Release, Moses enunciates and explains the ancient law regarding treatment of the poor.

A READING FROM THE BOOK OF DEUTERONOMY.

[v. 7: Begin "Moses addressed the people of Israel saying, 'If there is among you. . . .' "]

2 Corinthians 8:1–9, 13–15

At the time when a collection was being made for needy Christians in Jerusalem, Paul wrote this about stewardship to the church in Corinth.

A READING FROM THE SECOND EPISTLE TO THE CORINTHIANS.

Mark 5:22–24, 35b–43

This incident describes an unexpected aspect of the authority of Jesus as Lord.

A READING FROM THE GOSPEL OF MARK.

[v. 22: Omit "Then"; read "Jesus" instead of "him."]

Proper 9 (Closest to July 6)

Ezekiel 2:1–7

This vision convinced Ezekiel that God had chosen him to be spokesperson and prophet.

A READING FROM THE BOOK OF EZEKIEL.

[*Begin with 1:28: Read* "I had a vision of the glory of God, and when I saw it. . . ."]

2 Corinthians 12:2–10

Referring to himself as "a person in Christ," Paul gives us a glimpse of what he had to endure in order to carry on his ministry as the Lord's spokesperson.

A READING FROM THE SECOND EPISTLE TO THE CORINTHIANS.

Mark 6:1–6

During Jesus' ministry in Galilee, he returned to his hometown. This is how he was received.

A READING FROM THE GOSPEL OF MARK.

[*v. 1: Begin* "Jesus left the shores of Galilee and came to his hometown, Nazareth, and his disciples followed him."]

Proper 10 (Closest to July 13)

Amos 7:7-15

Amos had a prophetic vision that he obeyed but that got him in trouble. Here is his account of what happened.

A READING FROM THE BOOK OF AMOS.

[*v. 7: Begin* "This is what the Lord God showed me. . . ."]

Ephesians 1:1-14

The opening chapter of the Epistle to the Ephesians is essentially an outline of the writer's Christian belief.

A READING FROM THE EPISTLE TO THE EPHESIANS.

Mark 6:7-13

Midway through his ministry, Jesus sent his disciples out on their own as his emissaries. These were their instructions and their results.

A READING FROM THE GOSPEL OF MARK.

[*v. 7: Begin* "Jesus called the twelve and began. . . ."]

Proper 11 (Closest to July 20)

Isaiah 57:14b–21
In the poetry of Second Isaiah, we find these stanzas about God abiding with the chosen people. God's presence will have elements that fill us with both joy and trepidation.

A READING FROM THE BOOK OF ISAIAH.

Ephesians 2:11–22
Here the author of Ephesians explains the spiritual unity that binds members of the Christian Church together.

A READING FROM THE EPISTLE TO THE EPHESIANS.

[v. 11: Omit "So then."]

Mark 6:30–44
This is Mark's account of the feeding of the five thousand.

A READING FROM THE GOSPEL OF MARK.

Proper 12 (Closest to July 27)

2 Kings 2:1–15

One of the great storytellers of the Old Testament describes the transfer of authority from Elijah the prophet to his successor, Elisha.

A READING FROM THE SECOND BOOK OF KINGS.

Ephesians 4:1–7, 11–16

Here at the beginning of the ethical section of Ephesians, the author describes the behavior and contribution of members of the Christian church and the ultimate goal toward which they strive.

A READING FROM THE EPISTLE TO THE EPHESIANS.

Mark 6:45–52

This little incident occurred right after the feeding of the five thousand. Its significance for his followers was probably the awareness that Jesus was Lord even over the physical world.

A READING FROM THE GOSPEL OF MARK.

[*v. 45: Begin* "Immediately Jesus made. . . ."]

Proper 13 (Closest to August 3)

Exodus 16:2–4, 9–15

This is the account of how God fed the Israelites with manna in the wilderness. Christian liturgy is deeply rooted in this Old Testament idea of bread from heaven with which God feeds the people.

A READING FROM THE BOOK OF EXODUS.

Ephesians 4:17–25

This part of the ethical section of Ephesians sounds like a bit of early Christian preaching, which it probably was.

A READING FROM THE EPISTLE TO THE EPHESIANS.

John 6:24–35

Following the account of the feeding of the five thousand, John's gospel has an extended discourse on its meaning. This is part of it.

A READING FROM THE GOSPEL OF JOHN.

Proper 14 (Closest to August 10)

Deuteronomy 8:1–10
In this address to the children of Israel, Moses exhorts them to keep God's commandments in gratitude for God's goodness to them.

A READING FROM THE BOOK OF DEUTERONOMY.

[*v. 1: Begin* "Moses said. . . ."]

Ephesians 4: (25–29) 30—5:2
This exhortation to Christian behavior is in what may have been part of an early Christian sermon.

A READING FROM THE EPISTLE TO THE EPHESIANS.

[*v. 30: Omit* "And."]

John 6:37-51
This is part of the Lord's discourse on the significance of the feeding of the five thousand.

A READING FROM THE GOSPEL OF JOHN.

Proper 15 (Closest to August 17)

Proverbs 9:1–6

Here Wisdom is pictured as a prosperous housewife. The "simple" person referred to is one open to any influence.

A READING FROM THE BOOK OF PROVERBS.

Ephesians 5:15–20

The writer of this epistle sums up in these words his exhortation to have done with pagan ways.

A READING FROM THE EPISTLE TO THE EPHESIANS.

John 6:53–59

Here is the conclusion of the Lord's discourse on the inner meaning of the eucharist.

A READING FROM THE GOSPEL OF JOHN.

Proper 16 (Closest to August 24)

Joshua 24:1-2a, 14-25

Joshua succeeded Moses as the leader of the children of Israel. Near the end of his days, Joshua gave his final admonition to them.

A READING FROM THE BOOK OF JOSHUA.

[*v. 1: Omit* "Then." *In v. 2, read only* "and Joshua said to all the people." *In v. 14, omit* "Now therefore."]

Ephesians 5:21-33

In the ethical section of the Epistle to the Ephesians, the writer uses the relationship of Christ and his church as a model for husband-wife relations.

A READING FROM THE EPISTLE TO THE EPHESIANS.

John 6:60-69

Just as Joshua of old exhorted the Israelites to make a spiritual choice and commitment, so also Jesus offers a similar choice.

A READING FROM THE GOSPEL OF JOHN.

[*Add vv. 57-59 to the reading and begin:* "Jesus said, 'As the living Father. . . .' "]

Proper 17 (Closest to August 31)

Deuteronomy 4:1–9

Moses exhorts the Israelites to keep God's law, pointing out the privileges that are theirs because of God's nearness and concern for them.

A READING FROM THE BOOK OF DEUTERONOMY.

[*v. 1: Begin* "Moses said, 'Now, O Israel, give heed. . . .' "]

Ephesians 6:10–20

In the closing chapter of the Epistle to the Ephesians, the author exhorts the Christian to be a warrior equipped with the same spiritual armor the prophet of old had described as the armor of God.

A READING FROM THE EPISTLE TO THE EPHESIANS.

[*v. 10: Omit* "Finally."]

Mark 7:1–8, 14–15, 21–23

Judaism in Jesus' day was smothered by oral tradition that overlay the commandments. Here Jesus attacks this spiritually crippling development.

A READING FROM THE GOSPEL OF MARK.

[*v. 1: Substitute* "Jesus" *for* "him."]

131

Proper 18 (Closest to September 7)

Isaiah 35:4–7a
To the Babylonian exiles, the prophet sings of God's saving power.

A READING FROM THE BOOK OF ISAIAH.

[*v. 7a: Stop after* "springs of water."]

James 1:17–27
This reading sounds like part of a sermon written near the end of the first century.

A READING FROM THE EPISTLE TO JAMES.

Mark 7:31–37
Mark makes it clear that Jesus' ministry is the messianic fulfillment of Old Testament prophecy. The people's comment, "He has done all things well," literally means, "How exactly he fulfills prophecies."

A READING FROM THE GOSPEL OF MARK.

[*v. 31: Read* "Jesus returned from the region. . . ."]

Proper 19 (Closest to September 14)

Isaiah 50:4-9

In this servant poem from Isaiah, the writer may have been thinking of an individual or of the nation as a whole or of the coming Messiah. But New Testament writers saw in the words a description of the Lord's passion.

A READING FROM THE BOOK OF ISAIAH.

James 2:1-5, 8-10, 14-18

In this reading, the writer of the Epistle of James is dealing with the behavior of members in the first-century Christian church.

A READING FROM THE EPISTLE OF JAMES.

Mark 8:27-38

At the critical midway point of his ministry, Jesus asks the disciples about people's opinion of him—and about their own opinion of him. Here is what transpired.

A READING FROM THE GOSPEL OF MARK.

or Mark 9:14-29

Here the father of an afflicted child brings the boy to Jesus. In the ensuing dialogue, that father becomes every one of us, and his words become the prayer we can most honestly pray.

A READING FROM THE GOSPEL OF MARK.

[v. 14: Begin "When Jesus and his companions came to the other disciples."]

Proper 20 (Closest to September 21)

Wisdom 1:16—2:1 (6–11) 12–22

The Book of Wisdom contains this soliloquy by those who are faithless and unbelieving.

A READING FROM THE BOOK OF WISDOM.

[*v. 16: Omit* "But."]

James 3:16—4:6

The writer of the Epistle of James is an earnest, commonsense moralist who is wholly concerned with everyday conduct. This passage is a clear example of why that is the case.

A READING FROM THE EPISTLE OF JAMES.

Mark 9:30–37

In this reading, Jesus, for the second time, predicts his suffering and death. He then explains what this means for those who would be his disciples.

A READING FROM THE GOSPEL OF MARK.

[*v. 30: Read* "Jesus and his disciples went on from there and passed through Galilee."]

Proper 21 (Closest to September 28)

Numbers 11:4–6, 10–16, 24–29
Moses did not have an easy time leading the Israelites through the wilderness. Here is one example.

A READING FROM THE BOOK OF NUMBERS.

[*This more felicitous editing is recommended: Numbers 11:1a, 4b–6, 11, 14, 16–17, 24–29. In v. 1a, omit "when" and end with ". . . misfortunes." In v. 4b, begin with "and said . . . ."*]

James 4:7–12 (13—5:6)
This reading is from the latter part of the Epistle of James. It contains an almost random list of injunctions on Christian behavior.

A READING FROM THE EPISTLE OF JAMES.

Mark 9:38–43, 45, 47–48
Loyal followers are tempted to be jealous for their leader's reputation and to want to put down any potential rivals. Jesus' disciples showed this tendency.

A READING FROM THE GOSPEL OF MARK.

[*v. 38: Substitute* "Jesus" *for* "him."]

Proper 22 (Closest to October 5)

Genesis 2:18–24

In Genesis, there are two creation stories. In the second one, we have this account of the creation of man and woman. The point is that man and woman are a unit; they belong together.

A READING FROM THE BOOK OF GENESIS.

[*Add v. 7 to the appointed reading. In v. 7, omit "Then."*]

Hebrews 2:(1–8) 9–18

In chapter 1, the author of Hebrews has explained who Jesus Christ is. In this chapter, the author gives a preview of Jesus' work of salvation.

A READING FROM THE EPISTLE TO THE HEBREWS.

[*v. 9: Omit "but."*]

Mark 10:2–9

In Jesus' day, the Genesis story we heard was used to support monogamy. While monogamous marriage is certainly intended to be permanent, scholars say that the justification for divorce can neither be disproven or proven by this passage.

A READING FROM THE GOSPEL OF MARK.

Proper 23 (Closest to October 12)

Amos 5:6-7, 10-15

This is the heart of the message of the prophet Amos to the people of the prosperous nation of Israel.

A READING FROM THE BOOK OF AMOS.

[*v. 10: Change* "they" *to* "you." *In vv. 10, 12, and 15, change* "gate" *to* "courts."]

Hebrews 3:1-6

After showing that Jesus is the final and perfect revelation of God, this author goes on to show that Jesus is superior to Moses.

A READING FROM THE EPISTLE TO THE HEBREWS.

Mark 10:17-27 (28-31)

Jesus uses an encounter with one seeking his advice to warn against a barrier that can prevent us from trusting in God.

A READING FROM THE GOSPEL OF MARK.

[*v. 17: Read* "As Jesus was setting out on a journey. . . ."]

Proper 24 (Closest to October 19)

Isaiah 53:4–12

This is part of a sixth-century B.C. poem. It may describe an individual, such as Jeremiah, or perhaps the whole nation of Israel in exile; we do not know. To early Christians, it was seen as a description of the Lord's passion.

A READING FROM THE BOOK OF ISAIAH.

Hebrews 4:12–16

This reading from Hebrews is part of two sections. The first deals with the incisive nature of the Word of God; the second is about Jesus as the heavenly high priest.

A READING FROM THE EPISTLE TO THE HEBREWS.

[*v. 12: Omit* "Indeed."]

Mark 10:35–45

This is a conversation between Jesus and his disciples during their walk from Galilee to Jerusalem not long before his passion.

A READING FROM THE GOSPEL OF MARK.

[*Begin with v. 32a.*]

Proper 25 (Closest to October 26)

Isaiah 59:(1-4) 9-19

In this reading, the God of justice and truth speaks in stern poetry, through an eighth-century B.C. prophet, to people who flout God's will.

A READING FROM THE BOOK OF ISAIAH.

[Here is a suggested editing of the passage: Isaiah 59:(1-4) 9, 12-17, 19. If vv. 1-4 are not read, omit "Therefore" in v. 9.]

Hebrews 5:12—6:1, 9-12

This writer is unsure of the Christian maturity of those addressed in this epistle. The author's warm concern for them shines through.

A READING FROM THE EPISTLE TO THE HEBREWS.

Mark 10:46-52

The early church saw in this incident universal meaning. The blind man is seen as representing every groping Christian who comes to the Lord.

A READING FROM THE GOSPEL OF MARK.

[v. 46: Begin "Jesus and his disciples came. . . ."]

Proper 26 (Closest to November 2)

Deuteronomy 6:1–9
Right after giving the Israelites the Ten Commandments, this is what Moses said to them.

A READING FROM THE BOOK OF DEUTERONOMY.

[v. 1: Begin "Moses said to the people of Israel, 'Now this is. . . .' "]

Hebrews 7:23–28
In this reading, the author of Hebrews contrasts Jesus, the heavenly high priest, with the levitical priesthood of the Old Testament.

A READING FROM THE EPISTLE TO THE HEBREWS.

[Begin with v. 22, "Jesus has become the guarantee of a better covenant."]

Mark 12:28–34
Here Jesus gives the classic, brief summary of the Ten Commandments.

A READING FROM THE GOSPEL OF MARK.

[v. 28: Begin "One of the scribes came near and heard Jesus and the Sadducees disputing. . . ."]

Proper 27 (Closest to November 9)

1 Kings 17:8–16

This is one of the miracles associated with the memory of Elijah. The prophet goes to the village of Zarephath, and here is what happened.

A READING FROM THE FIRST BOOK OF KINGS.

[*v. 8: Read* "The word of the Lord came to Elijah. . . ."]

Hebrews 9:24–28

Earlier, the writer of Hebrews explained that Jesus is the eternal, heavenly high priest. Now he contrasts Jesus' priestly accomplishments with that of Israel's high priest.

A READING FROM THE EPISTLE TO THE HEBREWS.

Mark 12:38–44

Jesus' teaching often grew out of the situation at hand. Here the situation leads to teaching on the quality of one's giving.

A READING FROM THE GOSPEL OF MARK.

[*v. 38: Begin* "As he taught, Jesus said. . . ."]

Proper 28 (Closest to November 16)

Daniel 12:1–4a (5–13)

The Book of Daniel closes with this vision of the last days. It contains one of the earliest references to life after death in the Old Testament.

A READING FROM THE BOOK OF DANIEL.

Hebrews 10:31–39

The writer of Hebrews tells of the seriousness of Christian commitment.

A READING FROM THE EPISTLE TO THE HEBREWS.

Mark 13:14–23

Here is advice to Christians who may have to face some great catastrophic event. The gospel writer credits the words to Jesus, but they may have been colored by some later event like the fall of Jerusalem.

A READING FROM THE GOSPEL OF MARK.

Proper 29 (Closest to November 23)

Daniel 7:9–14

This ancient vision of heaven has New Testament significance. Jesus was the earthly incarnation of the heavenly human being, sometimes translated Son of man, described here. Much of the language of the Lord's Prayer is traceable to this passage.

A READING FROM THE BOOK OF DANIEL.

[*v. 13: Read* "I saw one like a son of man. . . ."]

Revelation 1:1–8

The Book of Revelation contains awesome visions of God and of the victorious, ascended Christ. Here is the way that book begins.

A READING FROM THE BOOK OF REVELATION.

John 18:33–37

This is part of the account of Jesus' trial before Pilate. Here Jesus calls attention to his eternal role.

A READING FROM THE GOSPEL OF JOHN.

or Mark 11:1–11

During Jesus' triumphal ride into Jerusalem on Palm Sunday, the shouts of the crowd unknowingly point to Jesus' eternal significance.

A READING FROM THE GOSPEL OF MARK.

YEAR C

First Sunday of Advent

Zechariah 14:4-9

This reading is part of a vision of the last days. The reference to the coming of the Lord makes it appropriate in the Advent season.

A READING FROM THE BOOK OF ZECHARIAH.

[*v. 4: Begin* "On that day the Lord's feet shall stand. . . ." *The reading becomes more intelligible if vv. 6-8 are omitted.*]

1 Thessalonians 3:9-13

This pastoral passage closes with a prayer for the Thessalonian Christians as they look forward to the return of the crucified and risen Christ. That is a dominant theme of the Advent season.

A READING FROM THE FIRST EPISTLE TO THE THESSALONIANS.

Luke 21:25-31

A central conviction of first-century Christians was that Christ would shortly return in glory as Judge. This passage from Luke's gospel is devoted to evidences of that coming great day.

A READING FROM THE GOSPEL OF LUKE.

[*v. 25: Begin* "Jesus said, 'There will be signs. . . .' "]

Second Sunday of Advent

Baruch 5:1-9
This poem foretells the return of the Babylonian exiles to their own land. It has something of the flavor of the Advent season as the poet sings of "the light of God's glory with mercy and righteousness."

A READING FROM THE BOOK OF BARUCH.

Philippians 1:1-11
The opening words of Paul's letter to the members of the church in Philippi are almost a prayer. The Advent flavor of the passage comes out in the words "I am confident of this, that the one who began a good work among you will bring it to completion by the day of Jesus Christ."

A READING FROM THE EPISTLE TO THE PHILIPPIANS.

Luke 3:1-6
With these words, Luke, the historian, carefully dates his account of when the Word of the Lord came to John the Baptist, the Advent figure who heralded Jesus' coming.

A READING FROM THE GOSPEL OF LUKE.

Third Sunday of Advent

Zephaniah 3:14–20
This bit of Old Testament prophetic writing has Christmas overtones for us when we hear it at this time of year.

A READING FROM THE BOOK OF ZEPHANIAH.

Philippians 4:4–7 (8–9)
Paul is writing from a Roman prison shortly before his death. These words, then, have the weight of a final admonition to his fellow Christians.

A READING FROM THE EPISTLE TO THE PHILIPPIANS.

Luke 3:7–18
This is the fullest account of the impact of John the Baptist's ministry on the people of his day as he prepared them for the coming of God's Messiah.

A READING FROM THE GOSPEL OF LUKE.

[*v. 7: Begin* "John said to the crowds. . . ."]

Fourth Sunday of Advent

Micah 5:2–4

This is part of a prophet's vision of a glorious future for his people. It becomes for us a prediction of the Lord's coming.

A READING FROM THE BOOK OF MICAH.

[*v. 2: Omit* "But."]

Hebrews 10:5–10

Here a first-century writer makes it clear that a new order of things begins with the coming of Jesus Christ.

A READING FROM THE EPISTLE TO THE HEBREWS.

[*v. 5: Begin* "When Christ came into the world. . . ."]

Luke 1:39–49 (50–56)

Here is the setting in which the Magnificat, one of the Bible's most lovely hymns, occurs. Hearing it is obviously appropriate on the eve of Christmas.

A READING FROM THE GOSPEL OF LUKE.

Christmas Day I

Isaiah 9:2–4, 6–7
The prophet wrote this poem about the Messiah who was to come. You decide how accurately he foresees the role Jesus was to fill.

A READING FROM THE BOOK OF ISAIAH.

Titus 2:11–14
This epistle was perhaps read in church to Christians living about a century after the crucifixion-resurrection.

A READING FROM THE EPISTLE TO TITUS.

Luke 2:1–14 (15–20)

THE NATIVITY STORY ACCORDING TO LUKE.

Christmas Day II

Isaiah 62:6–7, 10–12

Here are two stanzas describing the chosen people of God. The second pictures that people when the Messiah comes.

A READING FROM THE BOOK OF ISAIAH.

Titus 3:4–7

This advice to early Christian leaders becomes an appropriate sermonette when we hear it on this day.

A READING FROM THE EPISTLE TO TITUS.

[*v. 4: Omit* "But."]

Luke 2:(1–14) 15–20

Our thinking about Christmas centers in the angelic announcement to the shepherds and their visit to the Christ Child.

A READING FROM THE GOSPEL OF LUKE.

Christmas Day III

Isaiah 52:7-10
Here are stanzas from a poem that might be entitled "The Lord Has Become King." They are of a piece with our celebration of the birth of Christ the Savior.

A READING FROM THE BOOK OF ISAIAH.

[*v. 7: Begin* "Thus says the Lord."]

Hebrews 1:1-12
This epistle opens with a description of the incarnation of God's Son in terms of its eternal significance.

A READING FROM THE EPISTLE TO THE HEBREWS.

John 1:1-14
The Fourth Gospel opens with a description of the eternal significance of the coming of God's Son and of people's response to that coming. The meaning of "the Word" is pivotal. It embraces God's creative power, purpose, and wisdom.

A READING FROM THE GOSPEL OF JOHN.

153

First Sunday after Christmas

Isaiah 61:10—62:3
In this poem, an ancient seer sings of the glad tidings of salvation to Zion. Heard on this day, these words become part of the profound joy of this feast of Christ's nativity.

A READING FROM THE BOOK OF ISAIAH.

Galatians 3:23–25; 4:4–7
With the coming of Christ, our relation to God has changed from legalism to faith. The apostle explains what this change means.

A READING FROM THE EPISTLE TO THE GALATIANS.

[*Because verses have been skipped, change* "But" *to* "For" *in 4:4.*]

John 1:1–18
The author of the Fourth Gospel stands back from the Christmas event and views it both in relation to God's eternal purpose and in relation to humanity's response to Christ's coming.

A READING FROM THE GOSPEL OF JOHN.

Holy Name (January 1)

Exodus 34:1–8

When Moses had received the Ten Commandments from God on Mount Sinai, he went down, only to find the children of Israel worshiping a golden calf. In his anger, he broke the tablets on which the commandments were written. Now Moses goes up the mountain a second time to receive the commandments from God.

A READING FROM THE BOOK OF EXODUS.

Romans 1:1–7

This is the salutation with which the Epistle to the Romans begins. Here we see why zeal to proclaim the Lord's name among the nations dominated Paul's whole life.

A READING FROM THE EPISTLE TO THE ROMANS.

Luke 2:15–21

This part of the nativity story includes the account of the Jewish ceremony in which the baby Jesus received his name.

A READING FROM THE GOSPEL OF LUKE.

Second Sunday after Christmas

Jeremiah 31:7–14
This poem describes the return of the exiles to Zion.

Ephesians 1:3–6, 15–19a
The Epistle to the Ephesians opens with this thanksgiving, which describes what the coming of Jesus Christ is intended to mean in our lives.

Matthew 2:13–15, 19–23
This is the account of the flight of the Holy Family into Egypt.

[*v. 13: Substitute* "the Wise Men" *for* "they."]

or Luke 2:41–52
This is the only story in the gospels about Jesus' childhood.

[*v. 41: Substitute* "Jesus" *for* "his."]

or Matthew 2:1–12
This is the account of the Wise Men coming to worship the Christ Child.

The Epiphany (January 6)

Isaiah 60:1-6, 9
This bit of ancient poetry is filled with details we associate with the Wise Men's visit to the baby Jesus and also filled with the joy that is ours in the Epiphany season.

A READING FROM THE BOOK OF ISAIAH.

Ephesians 3:1-12
The Epiphany season rings with joy because Christ came as the Savior of all people, not just the Messiah of the Jews. In this reading, the apostle explains this Christian truth.

A READING FROM THE EPISTLE TO THE EPHESIANS.

Matthew 2:1-12
The story of the Wise Men sets forth the Epiphany message in picture pageantry.

A READING FROM THE GOSPEL OF MATTHEW.

First Sunday after Epiphany

Isaiah 42:1-9
This reading is one of a series of servant of the Lord poems in Second Isaiah. Regardless of who the author had in mind, the Christian identifies this description of the Lord's servant with Jesus.

A READING FROM THE BOOK OF ISAIAH.

Acts 10:34-38
This is part of Peter's speech to Cornelius, a Roman centurion, and his family, all of whom were eager to be baptized.

A READING FROM THE BOOK OF ACTS.

Luke 3:15-16, 21-22
The baptism of Jesus is a prominent Epiphany theme.

A READING FROM THE GOSPEL OF LUKE.

Second Sunday after Epiphany

Isaiah 62:1-5
The prophet-poet sings to the exiled and disgraced people of Israel of their coming freedom and vindication, describing that joyful day in terms of a marriage between God and God's people. This idea was built upon in the New Testament, and the church came to be called "the Bride of Christ."

A READING FROM THE BOOK OF ISAIAH.

1 Corinthians 12:1-11
God's gift of the Holy Spirit is the chief characteristic of the Christian church. Here Paul explains to the Christians in Corinth that the Spirit is also the motivating force in the lives of Christian individuals in their several callings.

A READING FROM THE FIRST EPISTLE TO THE CORINTHIANS.

John 2:1-11
The account of the marriage in Cana is an occasion when the glory of the Lord was revealed, which is a recurring Epiphany theme.

A READING FROM THE GOSPEL OF JOHN.

Third Sunday after Epiphany

Nehemiah 8:2–10
Ezra the priest reads the Book of the Law to the people of Jerusalem. This heritage of reverence for the Scriptures caused the Israelites to be called the People of the Book.

A READING FROM THE BOOK OF NEHEMIAH.

[v. 2: Omit "Accordingly." In v. 4, instead of the latter half beginning "and beside him. . . ," read "and beside him stood several prominent men of Israel to his right and to his left." In v. 7, instead of the proper names, read "Also appointed Levites helped the people . . . etc."]

1 Corinthians 12:12–27
This is Paul's classic pictorial description of the church as the Body of Christ.

A READING FROM THE FIRST EPISTLE TO THE CORINTHIANS.

Luke 4:14–21
In Luke's chronology of the events of Jesus' life, this synagogue incident happened at the beginning of Jesus' public ministry. The good news of God's salvation, talked about by the prophets, was now being experienced by people in what Jesus said and did.

A READING FROM THE GOSPEL OF LUKE.

Fourth Sunday after Epiphany

Jeremiah 1:4-10

This is known as "the call of Jeremiah." It is a description of his realization that he is destined to be God's spokesperson.

A READING FROM THE BOOK OF JEREMIAH.

1 Corinthians 14:12b-20

Among the manifestations of the Spirit's operation in the company of believers was the ability to speak in "various kinds of tongues" and to interpret tongues. This practice had gotten out of hand in the Corinthian church; here Paul deals with the matter.

A READING FROM THE FIRST EPISTLE TO THE CORINTHIANS.

Luke 4:21-32

In the Nazareth synagogue, Jesus explained ancient Scripture in terms of the current situation. This made his hearers angry. Here is what happened.

A READING FROM THE GOSPEL OF LUKE.

[v. 21: Begin "After reading Isaiah, Jesus began to say to them. . . ."]

Fifth Sunday after Epiphany

Judges 6:11–24a

This is the story of Gideon's dawning conviction that God wanted him to be a leader of his people.

A READING FROM THE BOOK OF JUDGES.

1 Corinthians 15:1–11

This is the earliest account we have of Christ's resurrection appearances—written about A.D. 55. Mark, the earliest gospel, was written about A.D. 70.

A READING FROM THE FIRST EPISTLE TO THE CORINTHIANS.

Luke 5:1–11

Some scholars believe that this Lucan incident is a misplaced resurrection appearance. In any case, because of the resurrection, Peter the fisherman would henceforth catch men and women.

A READING FROM THE GOSPEL OF LUKE.

Sixth Sunday after Epiphany

Jeremiah 17:5-10

Here in a poem, the prophet puts the message of the importance of trust in God in simple, easily understood analogies.

A READING FROM THE BOOK OF JEREMIAH.

1 Corinthians 15:12-20

In this reading, the apostle explains why he believes the resurrection of Christ is of central importance.

A READING FROM THE FIRST EPISTLE TO THE CORINTHIANS.

Luke 6:17-26

This is the opening part of Luke's Sermon on the Plain, which in a way parallels Matthew's Sermon on the Mount.

A READING FROM THE GOSPEL OF LUKE.

[*v. 17: Read* "Jesus came down with them. . . ."]

Seventh Sunday after Epiphany

Genesis 45:3–11, 21–28
This is the emotional scene when Joseph, food administrator of Egypt, made himself known to his brothers.

A READING FROM THE BOOK OF GENESIS.

1 Corinthians 15:35–38, 42–50
Here Paul thinks through the logic of the Christian's belief in the resurrection of Christ. This is the central portion of his argument.

A READING FROM THE FIRST EPISTLE TO THE CORINTHIANS.

Luke 6:27–38
This is the portion of Jesus' Sermon on the Plain that deals with the way a Christian treats others, especially enemies. Here is the Golden Rule in context.

A READING FROM THE GOSPEL OF LUKE.

[*v. 27: Begin* "Jesus said, 'I say to you. . . .' "]

Eighth Sunday after Epiphany

Jeremiah 7:1-7 (8-15)
Jeremiah's "temple sermon" is a collection of his important messages and has been called "Jeremiah's Sermon on the Mount."

A READING FROM THE BOOK OF JEREMIAH.

1 Corinthians 15:50-58
Here is the conclusion of Paul's chapter about the Lord's resurrection and ours.

A READING FROM THE FIRST EPISTLE TO THE CORINTHIANS.

Luke 6:39-49
This is the concluding part of Jesus' Sermon on the Plain.

A READING FROM THE GOSPEL OF LUKE.

[*v. 39: Begin* "Jesus told the crowd this parable. . . ."]

Last Sunday after Epiphany

Exodus 34:29–35

In the Bible, brightness is associated with God's glory. When Moses came down from Mount Sinai with the Ten Commandments, his face shone with the reflected glory of God.

A READING FROM THE BOOK OF EXODUS.

[*v. 35: Read* ". . . until he went in to speak with the Lord."]

1 Corinthians 12:27—13:13

This is Paul's great hymn describing and praising Christian love.

A READING FROM THE FIRST EPISTLE TO THE CORINTHIANS.

Luke 9:28–36

This incident is known as the transfiguration of Christ.

A READING FROM THE GOSPEL OF LUKE.

[*v. 28: Begin* "Now about eight days after Jesus first predicted his passion and death, he took with him. . . ."]

Ash Wednesday

Joel 2:1-2, 12-17

In about 400 B.C. the prophet Joel sees in a locust plague the ultimate judgment of God, the Day of the Lord. His call to repent is appropriately ours on Ash Wednesday.

A READING FROM THE BOOK OF JOEL.

or Isaiah 58:1-12

God, through an unknown ancient prophet, berates his people because their worship does not result in just and righteous behavior. His message is appropriate to our thinking as we enter the season of Lent.

A READING FROM THE BOOK OF ISAIAH.

[v. 1: Begin, "Thus says the Lord."]

2 Corinthians 5:20—6:10

Paul, using himself as an example, explains to Corinthian Christians the discipline of life and the endurance of suffering which being a follower of Christ entails.

A READING FROM THE SECOND EPISTLE TO THE CORINTHIANS.

[v. 20: Omit "So."]

Matthew 6:1-6, 16-21

In the Sermon on the Mount, Jesus teaches his followers the way in which their practice of piety will be acceptable to God.

A READING FROM THE GOSPEL OF MATTHEW.

[v. 1: Begin, "Jesus said."]

First Sunday in Lent

Deuteronomy 26:(1–4) 5–11

Israel's faith is grounded in history. So it is not surprising that this passage, used as part of formal, liturgical worship by the Jews, reviews that history in what might be considered Israel's creed.

A READING FROM THE BOOK OF DEUTERONOMY.

[*Read vv. 1, 5–11.*]

Romans 10:(5–8a) 8b–13

Biblical religion is spoken religion. Paul endorses this practice, which has characterized Israel's faith from the earliest days.

A READING FROM THE EPISTLE TO THE ROMANS.

Luke 4:1–13

This is Luke's account of our Lord's temptations in the wilderness. Notice that his defense against temptation lay in his familiarity with the Scriptures of his people.

A READING FROM THE GOSPEL OF LUKE.

Second Sunday in Lent

Genesis 15:1-12, 17-18

Biblical faith is grounded in the covenant God made with Abram. The described gruesome bit of ceremony was a primitive way of affirming an agreement.

A READING FROM THE BOOK OF GENESIS.

[v. 12: Read only "As the sun was going down, a deep sleep fell on Abram."]

Philippians 3:17—4:1

The New Testament is the record of the new covenant with God, which centers in Jesus Christ, the crucified and risen Lord. Paul succinctly describes this loyalty and its demand in terms of citizenship.

A READING FROM THE EPISTLE TO THE PHILIPPIANS.

Luke 13:(22-30) 31-35

Jesus explains how difficult it is to move from the old covenant relationship with God to the new and how the change is strongly resisted.

[If only vv. 31–35 are read, use the following introduction.]

Herod's desire to get his hands on Jesus the wonder-worker is as dangerous to Jesus as is the resistance of those who do not want the old regime upset.

A READING FROM THE GOSPEL OF LUKE.

Third Sunday in Lent

Exodus 3:1–15

The call of Moses is a pivotal event in Israel's history. As a result of it, Moses knew how God felt about the enslaved Israelites and that he, Moses, would have a role in their deliverance.

A READING FROM THE BOOK OF EXODUS.

1 Corinthians 10:1–13

Christianity is grounded in its Hebraic heritage. Here Paul explains why God was known as the Savior in former days and can be known so today.

A READING FROM THE FIRST EPISTLE TO THE CORINTHIANS.

Luke 13:1–9

In the course of his teaching, Jesus tells the parable of the vineyard, which throws light on the patience of God.

A READING FROM THE GOSPEL OF LUKE.

Fourth Sunday in Lent

Joshua (4:19–24); 5:9–12

This is the account of the end of the Israelites' trek through the wilderness from Egypt,
symbolized by the absence of manna from
heaven. The Passover celebrated the way in
which God had delivered them from Pharaoh's
bondage; it now had deeper significance.

A READING FROM THE BOOK OF JOSHUA.

2 Corinthians 5:17–21

Just as the Israelites were once making a
new beginning in the Promised Land, so the
Christian believer begins anew, a new creation,
as Christ's follower. This is the Christian's commission.

A READING FROM THE SECOND EPISTLE TO THE
CORINTHIANS.

[*v. 17: Omit* "So."]

Luke 15:11–32

The parable of the prodigal son.

A READING FROM THE GOSPEL OF LUKE.

[*v. 11: Begin,* "Jesus said. . . ."]

Fifth Sunday in Lent

Isaiah 43:16-21
To a nomadic people, water is life itself. God who saved the Israelites from death in the waters of the Red Sea now is their source of life by providing water for them in the wilderness. This poem might be called "Give My Chosen People Drink."

A READING FROM THE BOOK OF ISAIAH.

Philippians 3:8-14
Here Paul the apostle shares with the Christians at Philippi his attitude toward the suffering he has endured in carrying out his missionary vocation.

A READING FROM THE EPISTLE TO THE PHILIPPIANS.

[*v. 8: Omit* "More than that."]

Luke 20:9-19
In this parable of the tenants, Jesus warns the leaders of Israel that their violation of their intended role will result in his suffering and death.

A READING FROM THE GOSPEL OF LUKE.

[*v. 9: Begin,* "Jesus began to tell. . . ."]

Palm Sunday

Luke 19:29–40
Here is the account of the occasion from which Palm Sunday takes its name.

A READING FROM THE BOOK OF LUKE.

[*v. 29: Begin* "When Jesus had come. . . ."]

Isaiah 45:21–25
These verses are part of a poem in which God speaks through the prophet concerning the conversion of the nations.

A READING FROM THE BOOK OF ISAIAH.

[*v. 21: Begin* "Thus says the Lord. . . ."]

or Isaiah 52:13—53:12
This suffering servant poem is one of the spiritual high points of the Old Testament. It is a remarkable description of the meaning of Christ's passion, which was to take place centuries later.

A READING FROM THE BOOK OF ISAIAH.

Philippians 2:5–11
Here in a nutshell is Paul's belief about Jesus Christ.

A READING FROM THE EPISTLE TO THE PHILIPPIANS.

Luke (22:39–71) 23:1–49 (50–56)
The passion and death of Jesus Christ according to Luke.

A READING FROM THE GOSPEL OF LUKE.

173

Maundy Thursday

Exodus 12:1–14a
This is the origin of the Feast of the Passover, the symbolism of which lies behind the Lord's Supper.

A READING FROM THE BOOK OF EXODUS.

1 Corinthians 11:23–26 (27-32)
This is the earliest account of the institution of the Lord's Supper. Paul wrote to the Corinthian Christians almost two decades before the first gospel appeared.

A READING FROM THE FIRST EPISTLE TO THE CORINTHIANS.

John 13:1–15
This is the only account of the Last Supper in John's Gospel. Earlier, following the feeding of the five thousand, Jesus discusses what it means to "eat the flesh of the Son of Man and to drink his blood."

A READING FROM THE GOSPEL OF JOHN.

or Luke 22:14–30
This is Luke's account of the institution of the Lord's Supper.

A READING FROM THE GOSPEL OF LUKE.

[*v. 14: Read*, "When the hour had come, Jesus took his place. . . ."]

Good Friday

Isaiah 52:13—53:12
This is the best known of the servant of the Lord poems in Isaiah. Its deep spiritual insights have lead the Church to describe the Lord's passion in its phrases.

A READING FROM THE BOOK OF ISAIAH.

or Genesis 22:1–18
The story of Abraham's willingness to sacrifice his son at God's command and without losing faith in the goodness of God's eternal purposes, adds a dimension of meaning to the Lord's passion.

A READING FROM THE BOOK OF GENESIS.

[v. 1: Omit "After these things."]

or Wisdom 2:1, 12–24
This passage sounds like an elaboration of the thoughts of the high priest and his colleagues who were responsible for the Lord's passion and death.

A READING FROM THE BOOK OF WISDOM.

Hebrews 10:1–25
Here a New Testament writer seeks to explain the significance of the fact that the blood of Jesus was shed for us.

A READING FROM THE EPISTLE TO THE HEBREWS.

John (18:1–40) 19:1–37
THE PASSION OF OUR LORD JESUS CHRIST AC-CORDING TO JOHN.

Easter Day

Acts 10:34–43
Here is part of an early Christian sermon preached by Peter, the leading disciple, who was one of the first to see the risen Lord.

A READING FROM THE BOOK OF ACTS.

[*v. 34: Omit* "Then."]

or Isaiah 51:9–11
This is part of a poem on "the coming salvation." On this day when the prophet speaks of the joy of the redeemed of the Lord, we naturally think of believers in the risen Christ.

A READING FROM THE BOOK OF ISAIAH.

Colossians 3:1–4
Here is the effect belief in the risen Lord is meant to have on a Christian's life.

A READING FROM THE EPISTLE TO THE COLOSSIANS.

Luke 24:1–10
This is Luke's account of what took place that first Easter morning.

A READING FROM THE GOSPEL OF LUKE.

[*v. 1: Omit* "But."]

Easter Evening

Acts 5:29a, 30–32

Peter and the other apostles had defied the religious authorities by preaching that Jesus had risen from the dead. They were arrested and brought before the Sanhedrin. This was Peter's defense.

A READING FROM THE BOOK OF ACTS.

[*v. 29: Omit* "But."]

or Daniel 12:1–3

This vision from the Book of Daniel is the first clear mention in the Old Testament of a resurrection of the wicked as well as the righteous.

A READING FROM THE BOOK OF DANIEL.

1 Corinthians 5:6b–8

In the Passover ritual, unleavened bread was associated with the remembrance of Israel's redemption from Egypt—a people's new start. Here Paul transfers that ancient association to Christ's resurrection and the new start that is ours because of the risen Christ.

A READING FROM THE FIRST EPISTLE TO THE CORINTHIANS.

Luke 24:13–35

Luke's Easter evening account is significant because the ways those disciples knew the risen Lord are ours also.

A READING FROM THE GOSPEL OF LUKE.

[*v. 13: Begin* "Now on that same day two of Jesus' followers were going. . . ."]

Second Sunday of Easter

Acts 5:12a, 17–22, 25–29
This is the account of what happened on one of the first occasions when the apostles made public statements about the resurrection of Christ.

A READING FROM THE BOOK OF ACTS.

or Job 42:1–6
The drama of the Book of Job closes with Job's realization that God's plans and purposes are not capricious and arbitrary.

A READING FROM THE BOOK OF JOB.

[*v. 3: Begin* "You said." *And v. 4: Begin* "You said."]

Revelation 1:(1–8) 9–19
In the initial vision of John, the seer imprisoned on the island of Patmos, the risen and exalted Christ appears with a message to the churches.

A READING FROM THE BOOK OF REVELATION.

John 20:19–31
This is the Fourth Gospel account of what took place on the evening of the first Easter Day.

A READING FROM THE GOSPEL OF JOHN.

Third Sunday of Easter

Acts 9:1–19a

This event transformed Saul, the determined persecutor of Christians, into a Christian apostle.

A READING FROM THE BOOK OF ACTS.

or Jeremiah 32:36–41

At the time when Jerusalem was under seige and Jeremiah was in prison, he purchased a field in Anathoth, his hometown, which was behind enemy lines. His dramatic act of faith in the future of his nation was coupled with this message from God renewing the ancient covenant. Here, in a sense, is resurrection within history.

A READING FROM THE BOOK OF JEREMIAH.

[v. 36: Begin "Thus says the Lord. . . ."]

Revelation 5:6–14

This is a vision of the risen and glorified Christ that John the seer, prisoner on the island of Patmos, had in the first century.

A READING FROM THE BOOK OF REVELATION.

[The description is filled with majesty and awe. You are reading what Bach set to music. You may want to introduce it by reading 4:1a and 5:1 in order to set the stage.]

John 21:1–14

The crucifixion was disillusioning. The disciples were getting ready to return to their former way of life when the risen Christ came to them. Here is what happened.

A READING FROM THE GOSPEL OF JOHN.

179

Fourth Sunday of Easter

Acts 13:15-16, 26-33 (34-39)
Paul and Barnabas on their missionary travels attended the synagogue in Antioch of Pisidia. This is what happened.

A READING FROM THE BOOK OF ACTS.

or Numbers 27:12-23
This is the account of Moses commissioning Joshua to be his successor as the leader of the children of Israel.

A READING FROM THE BOOK OF NUMBERS.

Revelation 7:9-17
John the seer, prisoner in an island concentration camp, had this vision of the glorified martyrs in heaven.

A READING FROM THE BOOK OF REVELATION.

John 10:22-30
Jesus enlarges on his role as the Good Shepherd in this encounter with those who were hostile to him.

A READING FROM THE GOSPEL OF JOHN.

Fifth Sunday of Easter

Acts 13:44–52
The resurrection preaching of Paul in the synagogue at Antioch of Pisidia was so popular that he and Barnabas were invited to speak again the next week. This is what happened.

A READING FROM THE BOOK OF ACTS.

or Leviticus 19:1–2, 9–18
This is the passage from which Jesus got his love-your-neighbor commandment.

A READING FROM THE BOOK OF LEVITICUS.

Revelation 19:1, 4–9
John, the prisoner seer on the island of Patmos, has this heavenly vision. This and Ephesians 5:23–24 are the only New Testament passages in which the church is called the Bride of Christ, the Lamb of God.

A READING FROM THE BOOK OF REVELATION.

John 13:31–35
In his upper room discourses just before his passion, Jesus gave the disciples this new commandment.

A READING FROM THE GOSPEL OF JOHN.

[*v. 31: Begin* "When Judas had gone out. . . ."]

Sixth Sunday of Easter (Rogation Sunday)

Acts 14:8–18

On their missionary journey, Paul and Barnabas visit Lystra, a town in Asia Minor, in order to tell the people about Christ's resurrection. This is what happened.

A READING FROM THE BOOK OF ACTS.

or Joel 2:21–27

This prophecy is addressed to people who have suffered both drought and a plague of locusts.

A READING FROM THE BOOK OF JOEL.

[*v. 21: Begin* "Thus says the Lord. . . ."]

Revelation 21:22—22:5

In this reading, John the seer, imprisoned on the island of Patmos, tells of his vision of the New Jerusalem.

A READING FROM THE BOOK OF REVELATION.

John 14:23–29

Here Jesus reassures the disciples about what will happen when he is no longer physically present with them.

A READING FROM THE GOSPEL OF JOHN.

[*v. 23: Begin* "Jesus said. . . ."]

Ascension Day

Acts 1:1-11
Luke begins his Book of Acts with this description of Jesus' last resurrection appearance.

A READING FROM THE BOOK OF ACTS.

or 2 Kings 2:1-15
This Old Testament ascension story is part of the Elijah saga. It is the occasion of the transfer of authority from Elijah to Elisha.

A READING FROM THE SECOND BOOK OF KINGS.

Ephesians 1:15-23
The author of this epistle explains the significance of Christ's ascension to the Christians in Ephesus.

A READING FROM THE EPISTLE TO THE EPHESIANS.

Luke 24:49-53
Luke describes the Lord's ascension, his last resurrection appearance, twice—here at the end of his gospel and in the opening chapter of Acts. The promise of "power from on high"—the Lord's Spirit and continual presence—makes this an occasion of great joy.

A READING FROM THE GOSPEL OF LUKE.

[v. 49: Omit "And."]

or Mark 16:9-15, 19-20
This is Mark's account of the Lord's resurrection appearances and of his ascension.

A READING FROM THE GOSPEL OF MARK.

[v. 9: Read "Now after Jesus rose on the first day. . . ."]

Seventh Sunday of Easter

Acts 16:16-34

This is what happened to Paul and Silas in Philippi.

A READING FROM THE BOOK OF ACTS.

or 1 Samuel 12:19-24

This incident, in the closing days of Samuel's spiritual leadership of Israel, throws light on the importance of prayer for others.

A READING FROM THE FIRST BOOK OF SAMUEL.

Revelation 22:12-14, 16-17, 20

John the seer, a prisoner on the island of Patmos, closes his Book of Revelation, the last book of the Bible, with this vision of the risen Christ.

A READING FROM THE BOOK OF REVELATION.

[*v. 12: Begin* "The risen Lord said. . . ."]

John 17:20-26

Shortly before his passion and death, Jesus prayed for his disciples. This is the conclusion of that prayer.

A READING FROM THE GOSPEL OF JOHN.

[*v. 20: Add* "Jesus said. . . ."]

Day of Pentecost

Acts 2:1–11

The events of Pentecost catapulted the believers in the risen Christ into missionary activity. Here is the story.

A READING FROM THE BOOK OF ACTS.

or Joel 2:28–32

The prophet sees in a natural disaster the prototype of the coming day of the Lord when there will be an outpouring of God's Spirit.

A READING FROM THE BOOK OF JOEL.

[*v. 28: Add* "Thus says the Lord, 'I will pour out. . . .' "]

1 Corinthians 12:4–13

Paul describes the various gifts of the Spirit and their relation to one another.

A READING FROM THE FIRST EPISTLE TO THE CORINTHIANS.

John 20:19–23

This is John's account of what took place on that first Easter evening.

A READING FROM THE GOSPEL OF JOHN.

or John 14:8–17

In Jesus' upper room discourse with the disciples at the Last Supper, here is what he said about the Holy Spirit.

A READING FROM THE GOSPEL OF JOHN.

Trinity Sunday

Isaiah 6:1–8
Isaiah tells of the occasion when he became convinced that the Holy God had called him to be a prophet.

A READING FROM THE BOOK OF ISAIAH.

Revelation 4:1–11
This is the seer's vision of heaven. In it, we catch his feeling of awe before the majesty and holiness of God.

A READING FROM THE BOOK OF REVELATION.

John 16: (5–11) 12–15
In his upper room discourse, Jesus has this to say about the Holy Spirit.

A READING FROM THE GOSPEL OF JOHN.

[*v. 5 or 12: Begin* "Jesus said. . . ."]

Proper 1 (Closest to May 11)

Jeremiah 17:5-10

Here in a poem, the prophet puts the message of the importance of trust in God in simple, easily understood analogies.

A READING FROM THE BOOK OF JEREMIAH.

1 Corinthians 15:12-20

In this reading, the apostle explains why he believes the resurrection of Christ is of central importance.

A READING FROM THE FIRST EPISTLE TO THE CORINTHIANS.

Luke 6:17-26

This is the opening part of Luke's Sermon on the Plain, which in a way parallels Matthew's Sermon on the Mount.

A READING FROM THE GOSPEL OF LUKE.

[*v. 17: Begin* "Jesus came down the mountain with the twelve and stood on a level place. . . ."]

Proper 2 (Closest to May 18)

Genesis 45:3–11, 21–28
This is the emotional scene when Joseph, food administrator of Egypt, made himself known to his brothers.

A READING FROM THE BOOK OF GENESIS.

1 Corinthians 15:35–38, 42–50
Here Paul thinks through the logic of the Christian's belief in the resurrection of Christ. This is the central portion of his argument.

A READING FROM THE FIRST EPISTLE TO THE CORINTHIANS.

Luke 6:27–38
This is the portion of Jesus' Sermon on the Plain that deals with the way a Christian treats others, especially enemies. Here is the Golden Rule in context.

A READING FROM THE GOSPEL OF LUKE.

Proper 3 (Closest to May 25)

Jeremiah 7:1-7 (8-15)
Jeremiah's temple sermon is a collection of his important messages and has been called "Jeremiah's Sermon on the Mount."

A READING FROM THE BOOK OF JEREMIAH.

1 Corinthians 15:50-58
Here is the conclusion of Paul's chapter about the Lord's resurrection and ours.

A READING FROM THE FIRST EPISTLE TO THE CORINTHIANS.

Luke 6:39-49
This is the concluding part of Jesus' Sermon on the Plain.

A READING FROM THE GOSPEL OF LUKE.

[*v. 39: Begin* "Jesus told the crowd this parable. . . ."]

Proper 4 (Closest to June 1)

1 Kings 8:22–23, 27–30, 41–43

King Solomon built the Temple at Jerusalem. This was the king's prayer at its dedication.

A READING FROM THE FIRST BOOK OF KINGS.

Galatians 1:1–10

Paul and Barnabas had traveled through Galatia (part of present-day Turkey) establishing churches. Now those churches were foundering, so Paul writes to them.

A READING FROM THE EPISTLE TO THE GALATIANS.

Luke 7:1–10

In his encounter with Jesus, the Roman centurion recognizes in Jesus another man of authority but one whose authority reaches beyond this world, hence a matter of faith.

A READING FROM THE GOSPEL OF LUKE.

Proper 5 (Closest to June 8)

1 Kings 17:17-24
This is one of the wonder stories that came to be associated with the memory of Elijah the prophet.

A READING FROM THE FIRST BOOK OF KINGS.

[*v. 17: Begin* "The son of the widow of Zarephath in whose house Elijah was staying became ill; his illness was so severe. . . ."]

Galatians 1:11-24
The apostle Paul, in writing to the churches in Galatia, gives this autobiographical glimpse of his early years as a believer in the risen Christ.

A READING FROM THE EPISTLE TO THE GALATIANS.

Luke 7:11-17
Perhaps because of incidences like this, the words "the Lord, the giver of life" found their way into the Nicene Creed.

A READING FROM THE GOSPEL OF LUKE.

[*v. 11: Begin* "Jesus went. . . ."]

Proper 6 (Closest to June 15)

2 Samuel 11:26—12:10, 13–15

Here is a story about King David, the man, and Nathan, the man of God.

A READING FROM THE SECOND BOOK OF SAMUEL.

Galatians 2:11–21

In the early days of the Christian church, Jews who had become Christians found it hard to accept Gentile Christians as equals. Here Paul addresses this problem.

A READING FROM THE EPISTLE TO THE GALATIANS.

Luke 7:36–50

Here is the gospel in a nutshell. Surely the Heavenly Father is as compassionate and forgiving as Jesus.

A READING FROM THE GOSPEL OF LUKE.

Proper 7 (Closest to June 22)

Zechariah 12:8–10; 13:1

This is an ancient seer's vision of the victory of the Lord's people over the heathen in the day of the coming Messiah.

A READING FROM THE BOOK OF ZECHARIAH.

Galatians 3:23–29

In this reading, Paul explains that our oneness of faith in Jesus Christ wipes away all distinctions that usually separate us.

A READING FROM THE EPISTLE TO THE GALATIANS.

Luke 9:18–24

This incident is a watershed of insight in the lives of Jesus' disciples.

A READING FROM THE GOSPEL OF LUKE.

Proper 8 (Closest to June 29)

1 Kings 19:15–16, 19–21

God tells Elijah the prophet that Elisha is to be his successor. The casting of his mantle on Elisha is the symbolic transfer of authority, and Elisha's farewell meal with his family and friends is a religious celebration.

A READING FROM THE FIRST BOOK OF KINGS.

[*v. 15: Begin* "The Lord said to Elijah. . . ." *In v. 16, omit* "of Abelaholah" *and you will breathe easier.*]

Galatians 5:1, 13–25

In this reading, the apostle contrasts the qualities of life that distinguish those who are motivated by the Spirit of the risen Lord with the qualities of those who are not.

A READING FROM THE EPISTLE TO THE GALATIANS.

Luke 9:51–62

As Jesus heads for Jerusalem that last time, he lays down these challenging demands for those who would be his followers.

A READING FROM THE GOSPEL OF LUKE.

[*v. 51: Read* "When the days drew near for Jesus to be. . . ."]

Proper 9 (Closest to July 6)

Isaiah 66:10–16
The Book of Isaiah closes with a poem addressed to the Babylonian exiles. The restoration of Jerusalem and the coming messianic age are intertwined as the poet foresees a time of both comfort and of judgment.

A READING FROM THE BOOK OF ISAIAH.

[*v. 10: Begin* "Thus says the Lord, 'Rejoice. . . .' "]

Galatians 6:(1–10) 14–18
Paul closes his letter to the Christians in Galatia by reiterating his conviction that to be a Christian means to identify one's self with the crucified and risen Lord.

A READING FROM THE EPISTLE TO THE GALATIANS.

Luke 10:1–12, 16–20
Midway through his ministry, Jesus sends out teams of disciples to prepare people for his coming. These were his instructions to them, and this is what happened when they returned.

A READING FROM THE GOSPEL OF LUKE.

[*v. 1: Read* "The Lord appointed seventy. . . ."]

Proper 10 (Closest to July 13)

Deuteronomy 30:9–14

The Book of Deuteronomy is a series of addresses by Moses. This is part of one of his last addresses to the people of Israel.

A READING FROM THE BOOK OF DEUTERONOMY.

[*v. 9: Begin* "Moses summoned all the Israelites and said to them, 'The Lord your God. . . .' "]

Colossians 1:1–14

Paul had sent Epaphras to preach to the people of Colossae, a town near Ephesus. This is the opening part of the pastoral letter Paul now writes the members of that newly formed Christian congregation.

A READING FROM THE EPISTLE TO THE COLOSSIANS.

Luke 10:25–37

Jesus' parable of the good samaritan.

A READING FROM THE GOSPEL OF LUKE.

Proper 11 (Closest to July 20)

Genesis 18:1–10a (10b–14)
God had promised Abraham that his descendants would be numerous as the stars. At the time, the elderly couple, Abraham and Sarah, had no children. Here that divine promise begins to be fulfilled.

A READING FROM THE BOOK OF GENESIS.

Colossians 1:21–29
In this reading, Paul tells the Christians at Colossae something of his attitude toward the apostolic ministry and his part in it.

A READING FROM THE EPISTLE TO THE COLOSSIANS.

[*v. 21: Omit* "And."]

Luke 10:38–42
Here is a relaxed picture of Jesus in the home of intimate friends.

A READING FROM THE GOSPEL OF LUKE.

[*v. 38: Begin* "Now as Jesus and his disciples went on their way. . . ."]

Proper 12 (Closest to July 27)

Genesis 18:20–33
Here Abraham is talking with God; he haggles as he would in the marketplace. This is an example of the expression of reverent, persistent concern in one's dealing with God.

A READING FROM THE BOOK OF GENESIS.

Colossians 2:6–15
In this reading, Paul explains to the Christians at Colossae that the vital center of the Christian's life is the victorious Christ.

A READING FROM THE EPISTLE TO THE COLOSSIANS.

[*Consider omitting both v. 11 and the reference to circumcision in v. 13.*]

Luke 11:1–13
In Luke's Gospel, this is Jesus' major teaching about prayer.

A READING FROM THE GOSPEL OF LUKE.

[*v. 1: Begin* "Jesus was praying. . . ."]

Proper 13 (Closest to August 3)

Ecclesiastes 1:12–14; 2:(1–7, 11) 18–23

"The Preacher," as this writer calls himself, has had worldly success in acquiring many things, but now he is given over to despair and has become cynical.

A READING FROM THE BOOK OF ECCLESIASTES.

Colossians 3:(5–11) 12–17

In this reading, Paul tells the church members at Colossae what it means to be a Christian both in character and in conduct.

A READING FROM THE EPISTLE TO THE COLOSSIANS.

Luke 12:13–21

Jesus' parable of the rich fool makes us think about our attitude toward worldly possessions.

A READING FROM THE GOSPEL OF LUKE.

[v. 13: Begin "Someone in the crowd said to Jesus. . . ."]

Proper 14 (Closest to August 10)

Genesis 15:1–6

Abraham is called the father of the faithful (i.e., of faith-filled people). This little incident is part of the heritage that earned him that title.

A READING FROM THE BOOK OF GENESIS.

[*v. 1: Read* "The word of the Lord came. . . ."]

Hebrews 11:1–3 (4–7) 8–16

This reading is the opening part of a classic chapter on faith. It begins with a definition, then follows examples of great faith in the lives of individuals in Israel's history.

A READING FROM THE EPISTLE TO THE HEBREWS.

Luke 12:32–40

Here are a number of Jesus' sayings on the responsibilities and privileges of discipleship.

A READING FROM THE GOSPEL OF LUKE.

[*v. 32: Begin* "Jesus said, 'Do not be afraid. . . .' "]

Proper 15 (Closest to August 17)

Jeremiah 23:23–29

Here God through the prophet speaks out against false prophets. God can be stern as well as loving.

A READING FROM THE BOOK OF JEREMIAH.

[*v. 23: Begin* "Thus says the Lord of hosts, 'Am I a God . . . .' "]

Hebrews 12:1–7 (8–10) 11–14

This is one of the Bible's clearest discussions of God's sterner side; discipline is inherent in God's family.

A READING FROM THE EPISTLE TO THE HEBREWS.

[*v. 1: Omit* "Therefore."]

Luke 12:49–56

The fires of testing and of judgment are continual biblical themes. In this reading, these emphases are present, and we have a rare glimpse of the mind of Jesus that reveals some very mixed feelings.

A READING FROM THE GOSPEL OF LUKE.

[*v. 49: Begin* "Jesus said to his disciples, 'I came to bring fire. . . .' "]

Proper 16 (Closest to August 24)

Isaiah 28:14-22

In spite of the prophet's warning that only God can save them, the rulers of Jerusalem have made a secret political alliance with Egypt for protection from their enemies. This is the prophet's reaction.

A READING FROM THE BOOK OF ISAIAH.

[*v. 14: Omit "Therefore." Omitting vv. 19–21 makes the meaning of the passage clearer.*]

Hebrews 12:18-19, 22-29

This first-century Christian writer, in the manner of an Old Testament prophet, voices a warning to the church of that day. These stern words of warning and doom are coupled with a note of assurance.

A READING FROM THE EPISTLE TO THE HEBREWS.

Luke 13:22-30

Jesus is making his last trip to Jerusalem. His thoughts hover around the seriousness of being one of his followers.

A READING FROM THE GOSPEL OF LUKE.

Proper 17 (Closest to August 31)

Ecclesiasticus 10:(7–11) 12–18

Here an ancient sage has this to say about pride.

A READING FROM THE BOOK OF ECCLESIASTICUS.

Hebrews 13:1–8

Here are part of the closing words of an early Christian epistle. They give a picture of the level of behavior to which Christians aspired in the second generation of the Christian era.

A READING FROM THE EPISTLE TO THE HEBREWS.

Luke 14:1, 7–14

In this reading, Jesus tells two parables at a dinner party that draw lessons from familiar party behavior.

A READING FROM THE GOSPEL OF LUKE.

Proper 18 (Closest to September 7)

Deuteronomy 30:15–20
Moses concludes an address to the Israelites in the wilderness with these stern words of exhortation.

A READING FROM THE BOOK OF DEUTERONOMY.

[*v. 15: Begin* "Moses summoned all the Israelites and said to them. . . ."]

Philemon 1–20
Onesimus, a runaway slave, had become a Christian and was voluntarily returning to his master. Paul gave him this letter to give to his master.

A READING FROM THE EPISTLE TO PHILEMON.

Luke 14:25–33
The Semitic way of saying "I prefer this to that" is to say, "I like this and hate that." Jesus is here teaching about absolute commitment to the kingdom of God; other ties must not interfere.

A READING FROM THE GOSPEL OF LUKE.

[*Begin* "Now large crowds were traveling with Jesus. . . ."]

Proper 19 (Closest to September 14)

Exodus 32:1, 7–14

Intertwined with the account of the giving of the Ten Commandments at Mount Sinai is the story of the golden calf. In it, Moses is pictured as the great intercessor pleading for the welfare of his fellow Israelites.

A READING FROM THE BOOK OF EXODUS.

1 Timothy 1:12–17

In this biographical glimpse, Paul reveals how great a part God's mercy and forgiveness had played in his life.

A READING FROM THE FIRST EPISTLE TO TIMOTHY.

Luke 15:1–10

The Pharisees thought God's mercy did not extend beyond certain narrow limits. Jesus refutes this in his parables and cites two ways the lost receive mercy and are brought back.

A READING FROM THE GOSPEL OF LUKE.

Proper 20 (Closest to September 21)

Amos 8:4–7 (8–12)

To Amos the prophet, God was above all else the God of justice. In this oracle, he speaks out against the evil practices he sees in the marketplace.

A READING FROM THE BOOK OF AMOS.

[*For a more poignant ending, add v. 8a:* "Shall not the land tremble on this account?"]

1 Timothy 2:1–8

In this reading, Paul is giving fatherly advice to Timothy, who has become a leader in the second-generation Christian church.

A READING FROM THE FIRST EPISTLE TO TIMOTHY.

Luke 16:1–13

Jesus urges his followers to be serious about their religious calling. His parable is advocating farsightedness, not dishonesty.

A READING FROM THE GOSPEL OF LUKE.

[*v. 1: Begin* "Jesus said to his disciples. . . ."]

Proper 21 (Closest to September 28)

Amos 6:1–7

In God's name, the prophet Amos denounces the blinding pride that shuts people off from God and the self-indulgence that insulates them from compassion for those in need.

A READING FROM THE BOOK OF AMOS.

[*v. 1: Begin* "Thus says the Lord. . . ." *Because v. 2 is difficult and distracting, read only this edited version:* "Are you better than other kingdoms?"]

1 Timothy 6:11–19

This reading contains pastoral advice to a leader of the second-generation Christian church.

A READING FROM THE FIRST EPISTLE TO TIMOTHY.

[*v. 11: Read* "As for you, man of God, shun. . . ."]

Luke 16:19–31

This is Jesus' parable of the rich man and Lazarus, a parable of warning and guidance.

A READING FROM THE GOSPEL OF LUKE.

[*v. 19: Begin* "Jesus said. . . ."]

Proper 22 (Closest to October 5)

Habakkuk 1:1–6 (7–11) 12–13; 2:1–4
The prophet Habakkuk is deeply troubled by the prevalence of violence and strife, yet he is confident in God's righteousness and holiness. Here he wrestles with this dilemma and finally the answer comes.

A READING FROM THE BOOK OF HABAKKUK.

[*v. 5: Begin* "Thus says the Lord." *Note that vv. 5–6 belong in quotation marks.*]

2 Timothy 1:(1–5) 6–14
In this reading, the writer gives fatherly advice to Timothy, a second-generation leader in the Christian church.

A READING FROM THE SECOND EPISTLE TO TIMOTHY.

[*v. 6: Omit* "For this reason. . . ."]

Luke 17:5–10
Here are some of Jesus' comments on faith and responsibility.

A READING FROM THE GOSPEL OF LUKE.

Proper 23 (Closest to October 12)

Ruth 1:(1–7) 8–19a
The poignant story of Ruth is filled with the gratitude of a foreigner.

A READING FROM THE BOOK OF RUTH.

[*Read the entire lection (vv. 1–19a). Any summary of vv. 1–7 is likely to be inferior and almost as long as the original.*]

2 Timothy 2:(3–7) 8–15
In this reading, Paul gives fatherly advice to Timothy, a second-generation leader in the Christian church.

A READING FROM THE SECOND EPISTLE TO TIMOTHY.

Luke 17:11–19
Here is a little encounter filled with compassion and gratitude.

A READING FROM THE GOSPEL OF LUKE.

Proper 24 (Closest to October 19)

Genesis 32:3–8, 22–30

Jacob had tricked Esau out of his birthright and had fled the country to avoid Esau's wrath. Now Jacob, who had always gotten what he wanted by devious means, was returning. This is what happened.

A READING FROM THE BOOK OF GENESIS.

2 Timothy 3:14—4:5

In this reading, Paul gives advice to Timothy, a second-generation Christian leader.

A READING FROM THE SECOND EPISTLE TO TIMOTHY.

[*Begin 3:14* "Continue in what you have learned. . . ."]

Luke 18:1–8a

This parable of Jesus' causes us to think about our own praying in very human terms.

A READING FROM THE GOSPEL OF LUKE.

[*v. 1: Begin* "Jesus told them a parable. . . ."]

Proper 25 (Closest to October 26)

Jeremiah 14:(1–6) 7–10, 19–22

In a time of drought, the prophet Jeremiah pleads with God passionately in this prayer of confession of sin.

A READING FROM THE BOOK OF JEREMIAH.

2 Timothy 4:6–8, 16–18

These might be considered Paul's dying words. They are addressed to Timothy, a second-generation Christian leader.

A READING FROM THE SECOND EPISTLE TO TIMOTHY.

Luke 18:9–14

This parable of Jesus' causes us to evaluate the quality of our own praying.

A READING FROM THE GOSPEL OF LUKE.

[v. 9: Begin "Jesus told this parable. . . ."]

Proper 26 (Closest to November 2)

Isaiah 1:10-20

Through the prophet, God pleads with the people of Israel to turn from their religious insincerity and accept divine forgiveness.

A READING FROM THE BOOK OF ISAIAH.

2 Thessalonians 1:1-5 (6-10) 11-12

The Christians at Thessalonica were suffering persecution. This epistle of Paul's opens with a prayer of thanksgiving for their faith and words of reassurance.

A READING FROM THE SECOND EPISTLE TO THE THESSALONIANS.

Luke 19:1-10

Jesus was on his way to Jerusalem for the last time. Enroute he passed through Jericho. This encounter took place.

A READING FROM THE GOSPEL OF LUKE.

[v. 1: Read "Jesus entered Jericho. . . ."]

Proper 27 (Closest to November 9)

Job 19:23–27a
In this drama, Job has now reached the depths of despair and loneliness. He bursts forth in what has been called "the most momentous expression of faith . . . in the Bible."

A READING FROM THE BOOK OF JOB.

[*v. 25: In Hebrew, "know" is very emphatic. End v. 27a with ". . . and not another."*]

2 Thessalonians 2:13—3:5
Paul the apostle was a true evangelist. Here in a letter to members of the church he founded in Thessalonica, we catch something of his watchful care and loving concern.

A READING FROM THE SECOND EPISTLE TO THE THESSALONIANS.

[*v. 13: Omit "But."*]

Luke 20:27 (28–33) 34–38
Part of the cause of opposition to Jesus was his belief in life after death. The Sadducees did not share this belief and sought to embarrass him. Jesus accepts their challenge and explains his position.

A READING FROM THE GOSPEL OF LUKE.

Proper 28 (Closest to November 16)

Malachi 3:13—4:2a, 5-6

In the name of the Lord, the prophet Malachi addresses those who see no good in serving God. Then, as God's spokesperson, he speaks to the faithful about the coming day of retribution.

A READING FROM THE BOOK OF MALACHI.

2 Thessalonians 3:6-13

Paul was a tireless missionary. Here we see a bit of his work ethic.

A READING FROM THE SECOND EPISTLE TO THE THESSALONIANS.

Luke 21:5-19

Near the end of his ministry, Jesus foresees both a historic crisis within a generation and a final crisis at the end of history. He gives this advice to those who would be faithful to him.

A READING FROM THE GOSPEL OF LUKE.

Proper 29 (Closest to November 23)

Jeremiah 23:1–6

As God's spokesperson, the prophet Jeremiah condemns the people's leaders who have failed in their responsibilities. Then he tells of the glorious day when God's Messiah will reign as king.

A READING FROM THE BOOK OF JEREMIAH.

Colossians 1:11–20

In this reading, Paul tells the members of the church at Colossae what it means to be a Christian believer and how they are to think of Christ the Son of God.

A READING FROM THE EPISTLE TO THE COLOSSIANS.

Luke 23:35–43

We see Jesus on the cross apparently defeated, but that cross was soon to be the doorway to victory for the risen Christ.

A READING FROM THE GOSPEL OF LUKE.

[*v. 35: Begin* "The people stood by watching, but the rulers scoffed at Jesus, saying. . . ."]

or Luke 19:29–38

When Jesus rode into Jerusalem on Palm Sunday, the shouts of adoration were prophetic of the Lord's ultimate reign in glory.

A READING FROM THE GOSPEL OF LUKE.

[*v. 29: Begin* "When Jesus had come near. . . ."]

HOLY DAYS

The Presentation (February 2)

Malachi 3:1–4

This passage is usually associated in our thinking with John the Baptist, but because it speaks of "an offering . . . pleasing to the Lord," we hear it on this Feast of the Presentation of the Christ Child in the Temple.

A READING FROM THE BOOK OF MALACHI:

[*v. 1: Begin* "Thus says the Lord. . . ."]

Hebrews 2:14–18

In describing the Lord's work of salvation, the author of this epistle says "he had to be made like his brethren in every respect." This was true from the beginning, for his parents brought him to the Temple to present him to the Lord as the Law required of every firstborn Hebrew male child.

A READING FROM THE EPISTLE TO THE HEBREWS.

Luke 2:22–40

This is the account of the ceremony in which every firstborn Hebrew boy and his parents took part on his fortieth day.

A READING FROM THE GOSPEL OF LUKE.

219

The Transfiguration (August 6)

Exodus 34:29-35

This is the account of Moses' return from the mountaintop where he has received the Ten Commandments from God. Great light is associated with God's presence and God's reflected glory in individuals.

A READING FROM THE BOOK OF EXODUS.

2 Peter 1:13-21

This is a bit of early church writing in a time when Christian witness was being doubted. It shows the Lord's transfiguration to be a pivotal experience in the lives of Peter and his companions.

A READING FROM THE SECOND EPISTLE OF PETER.

Luke 9:28-36

This spiritual experience is known as the transfiguration of Christ.

A READING FROM THE GOSPEL OF LUKE.

[*v. 28: Begin* "Now about eight days after Peter had put into words the disciples' conviction that Jesus was the Messiah, Jesus took with him Peter. . . ."]

All Saints' Day (November 1)

Ecclesiasticus 44:1-10, 13-14
In the wisdom literature of the Apocrypha, we find this paean listing those whom the wise old author thought should be remembered gratefully on an occasion like All Saints' Day.

A READING FROM THE BOOK OF ECCLESIASTICUS.

[*To remove sex bias, in v. 1, read* "Let us now praise famous people and our ancestors in their generations." *In v. 3, read* ". . . and were individuals renowned for their power." *In v. 6, read* ". . . rich men and women furnished with resources." *In v. 8, read* ". . . so that we declare their praise." *And in v. 10, read* "But these were people of mercy." *If written in the margin, these changes can be done smoothly.*]

Revelation 7:2-4, 9-17
The seer imprisoned on the island of Patmos put his message of consolation and hope to fellow persecuted Christians in this vision.

A READING FROM THE BOOK OF REVELATION.

Matthew 5:1-12
The Sermon on the Mount begins with these beatitudes.

A READING FROM THE GOSPEL OF MATTHEW.

SCRIPTURE INDEX

Scripture Index